IT'S JUST ABOUT CHRISTMAS

IT'S JUST ABOUT *Christmas*

from *Today's Christian Woman* magazine

Compiled by

RAMONA CRAMER TUCKER

Tyndale House Publishers, Inc.

WHEATON, ILLINOIS

Library of Congress Cataloging-in-Publication Data

It's just about Christmas / compiled by Ramona Cramer Tucker.
    p. cm.
   "From the pages of Today's Christian woman."
   ISBN 0-8423-7075-7 (alk, paper)
   1. Christmas—United States. 2. United States—Religious life and customs. 3. United States—Social life and customs.
I. Tucker, Ramona, date. II. Today's Christian woman.
GT4986.A1177 1996
394.2'663'0973—dc20

96-7859

Printed in the United States of America

00 99 98 97 96
10 9 8 7 6 5 4 3 2 1

Presented To

_____

By

_____

Date

_____

Contents

Introduction

*O*nce again it's Christmas! As houses and apartments fill with the heady smells of pine and pie, the golden glow of candles in frosty windows, and the happy sounds of carolers, we know the holiday season is in full swing.

For many of us, the word *Christmas* is synonymous with joy—and also stress. We are bombarded with more decisions than at any other time of year. We wonder, Where should we go for Christmas? Mom's? Grandpa's? A friend's? Stay at home? What should we give as gifts that won't break our bank account? How can we sandwich holiday activities into our already busy days? When and how can we say no to overcommitment? Does having a "hospitable" home for the holidays mean we must imitate Martha Stewart?

All of these questions—and more—are why *It's Just About Christmas* was written: to answer your questions and give you hope and help for the season. Sections on home and family, food, gift giving, hospitality, traditions, and restoring the joy and meaning of Christmas offer

- practical encouragement
- easy "how to" guides
- gift giving ideas, including creative ones for those on tight budgets
- suggestions from well-known people such as Amy Grant, Rachael Crabb, Susan Ashton, and Marilyn Quayle on how they make the holidays special
- favorite recipes
- traditions with a twist
- humorous stories and cartoons
- and much, much more

Use the stories and ideas enclosed as a jumping-off point to spark and then record your own memories and brainstorms for a holiday season perfectly suited to *you* and your loved ones.

And this year, as you're "trying to do it all," it may be helpful to remember that Christmas is not about *things* but about *people*—and particularly one Person. For Jesus Christ, the Son of God, came from heaven to be born in an ordinary manger so that we might find peace and forgiveness not only on Christmas but every day of the year.

So, as we unwrap our gifts and enjoy our feasts and loved ones, let's give thanks for the greatest gift of all: God's Son.

Ramona Cramer Tucker
Editor, *Today's Christian Woman*

There's No Place like Home

What does *home* mean to you? Your parents'
home? Grandparents' farm? Your apartment? As
you head into this Christmas season, you may
be looking forward to gathering with your
extended family, getting together for a fun day
with friends, or perhaps enjoying a quiet day of
reading in front of the fireplace. But wherever
"home" is, and whatever "family" means to you,
this Christmas can be just the beginning of
crafting a one-of-a-kind celebration, perfectly
suited to you and those you love.

Some people think of Christmas as a lot of parties, but my husband, Gary, and I are hermits. We love being with our friends, but we don't go to a hundred Christmas parties. All through the winter, we have a fire burning in the fireplace from early morning until we go to bed, and we just enjoy being together as a family, listening to good music, and making . . . garlands out of construction paper rings to wrap around the tree. We get gorgeous, tall trees, but they look horrible because I want the kids to have fun decorating them.

Amy Grant

The Last Christmas

BABBIE MASON, as told to Holly G. Miller

As far back as I can remember, our entire family life revolved around the Lily Baptist Church in Jackson, Michigan—the church my dad founded and served as pastor for forty years. Dad and I were especially close since we shared in the church's ministry. He was in the pulpit, and I was at the piano (at first playing only in one key) for sixteen of those forty years.

My father was all things to all people. He was a pastor, county commissioner, president of the NAACP, host of a live radio broadcast every Sunday morning from the church, and teacher at the local college. To me, he was father, mentor, and hero.

Even after I had moved away from home, Christmas always reunited us, and a big part of those reunions took place at church. But of all our gatherings, the year that stands out from the others was December 1986, the last Christmas we were all together. Our whole family was there—Mom, Dad, my three brothers, my sister from Detroit, and the grandchildren. At that time, we had no idea we were celebrating Dad's last Christmas—that three months later he would die of a heart attack. As always, our day began with a sunrise community church service. By midmorning, my sister and I were sitting around the family's kitchen table, dicing celery, onions, and peppers under the ever watchful eye of our mom.

That day, Mom fixed everything from soul food to leg of lamb. Dinner was served in the dining room on the best china, and Dad was at the head of the table to bless the food. Afterward, we all went into the big family room where Dad dozed in his favorite rocking chair and the guys "coached" the football games on television. We all felt as though we were kids again.

The next year was very different and very difficult. Despite my dad's death, our family decided to gather at our parents' home and celebrate as we always had. Some traditions deserve to be maintained—no matter how the circumstances in our lives change.

Now, each Christmas becomes a little easier than the last. Our family makes a real effort to get together. In fact, we make *more* of an effort today because we realize that it's impossible to know what the new year might hold. We look on the holidays with joy and anticipation, although there's an empty spot in our hearts and a missing face at the head of the table. We know our loss is heaven's gain.

Traditions WITH A TWIST

Although my grandmother emigrated from Norway in her teens, I grew up with little understanding of my heritage. So several years ago, I attempted to restore those traditions to our family in a special Christmas Eve celebration.

After much research, Operation Norwegian Christmas began. I baked seven varieties of Norwegian Christmas cookies, then secretly sewed traditional *bunaden* (folkwear) vests for the men, and vests, aprons, and caps for the women. And I decorated a small tree with miniature Norwegian flags and handmade traditional ornaments.

The day finally arrived. My family came to Christmas Eve supper dressed according to my instructions to wear white shirts and black pants or skirts. They each found at their place setting a package containing his or her traditional outfit.

The meal was a success. Each new taste or sight reminded Dad of another story from childhood. We were treated with memories for several hours.

Over the years, we've added various elements to our celebration—and gained a deeper love of our family and our heritage.

MARSHA BELSAAS

Whose Home for the Holidays?
Dr. Diane Mandt Langberg

Question: *I've been remarried for two years, and we each brought one child into the relationship. As a result, we have many family members—and former family members—to appease at the holidays, and the time is fraught with tension. How can we handle this more constructively?*

Answer: It sounds as if competition over your family time is keen and as if your nuclear family is getting lost in the shuffle. You need to refocus on the family you and your spouse have made together—and consider your needs and desires during the holiday season. Delineate the values you and your spouse want to protect—otherwise, you'll find yourselves doing what everyone else wants and resenting it.

Once you've figured out what's important to your nuclear family, you need to consider what your extended families expect. Then figure out what you realistically can and cannot do. Keep in mind you don't have to meet everyone's expectations every year. You may need to see some people alternate years or alternate between Thanksgiving and Christmas.

As you and your spouse sort this out, listen carefully to what's important to each of you and look for ways to honor that. Your attitude toward each other as you make decisions is as important as the choices you make. Remember, the family you two have made needs to be treated with importance and respect.

Celebrate Advent at Home

KATHY BENCE

Advent, the time of spiritual preparation before the celebration of Christ's birth, begins on the fourth Sunday before Christmas. Here's how you and your family can make the four weeks of Advent a special celebration and part of your Christmas worship:

1. Make an Advent wreath.
If you live near evergreens, go out as a family and cut some branches. Go to a craft store and buy a wire wreath frame. Lay the frame on a plate and cover it with the greens. Put four pink candles in the wire holders, and place a large purple candle in the center of the wreath.

2. As a family, study the symbolism of each candle.
Week 1—The Prophecy candle represents the prophecies concerning the Messiah's birth.
   Read Malachi 3:1-4, and light the first pink candle.
Week 2—The Bethlehem candle represents the birthplace of the King.
   Read Micah 5:2, and light two pink candles.
Week 3—The Shepherd candle represents the joy of the shepherds.
   Read Luke 2:8-20, and light three pink candles.
Week 4—The Angel candle represents the part the angels played in Jesus' birth.
   Read Luke 1:26-38, and light the four pink candles.

   The Christ candle celebrates the coming of the Christ child. On Christmas Day light all five candles, and read together the account of Jesus' birth recorded in Luke 2. Then sing "O Come, All Ye Faithful."

3. Sing Christmas carols together every night at supper and especially on Sundays with your Advent candlelighting.

4. Read an Advent Scripture passage every evening for the month of December, using the following guide:

WEEK 1	WEEK 2	WEEK 3:	WEEK 4:
Malachi 3:1-4	Micah 5:2	Psalm 89:1-29	Matthew 3:1-3, 11-17
Mark 1:1-13	Isaiah 55	Luke 1:39-56	Rev. 1:10-18
Isaiah 40:1-11	Isaiah 9:2-7	Jeremiah 33:7-16	Luke 1:5-17
Isaiah 35	Matthew 2:1-12	Isaiah 61	Luke 1:18-25
John 1:1-10	Matthew 2:13-18	Luke 1:57-80	Christmas Day:
John 1:11-18	Matthew 2:19-23	Rev. 21:1-7	Luke 2:1-20
Isaiah 53:1-6	Isaiah 42:1-9	Luke 2:21-35	Luke 2:21-35
			Luke 2:36-40

Christmas Day: Luke 2:1-20

Happy Get-Togethers

KAREN HEFFNER

Experience tells us that family reunions are not always as happy as we would like. Here are some suggestions to minimize stress and maximize pleasure:

If the clan is coming to your house, plan sleeping arrangements in advance. Family members are more cooperative if they know they're going to have to share (or give up) their rooms for a few nights.

If age or handicap means guests will need special attention, discuss this with your family before the guests arrive. There's less chance of inadvertent thoughtlessness if you're prepared for things like Great-grandma's memory loss. If a family member will need to provide extra services such as baby-sitting, *ask* first and diminish resentment.

If you're the host, have a few things in mind to entertain guests, but be flexible. You needn't have every minute planned; interests vary, and guests might also appreciate the opportunity to rest a bit before setting out on a whirlwind of activity.

If you're the traveler, consider your hosts' schedule if they must meet you at the airport. If you don't travel the day before the holiday, you'll avoid probable delays.

Considerate guests pick up after themselves, help with chores, and (especially if they're staying for a while) offer to share the cost of groceries or dinners out. Both guests and hosts need private time. Sensitive people quietly retire to their rooms or go out for a walk or drive.

Family reunions—especially those at the holidays—hold the hope for renewed friendships and reconciliation. Unfortunately, things don't always work out as we wish. If we can bring our disappointment before the Lord, he can give us peace in the midst of tension.

Traditions WITH A TWIST

When I was a child, we celebrated Jesus' birthday with a specially made cake on Christmas morning. We sang "Happy Birthday" to Jesus and then dumped all our saved-up coins from our piggy banks onto the floor. We would count up the money and then go out and buy food for a needy neighbor or put it into the offering plate at church the next week.

EVANGELINE F. SCHOCK

"I thought the family-rental rate was too good to be true."

When You Can't Go Home

DENISE TURNER

Each year it gets more difficult and expensive for extended families to get together for the holidays. Even if you aren't able to go home for Christmas, there still are ways to make everyone's celebration a merry one.

Take advantage of video. You can tape the entire Christmas celebration for a relative who couldn't join you. Capture the mad rush of Christmas morning on film, add a few family skits, and include a pre-holiday tradition or two. If you aren't the video type, send a memory album that notes the high points of the season and fill it with kid-inspired photos and messages.

Set up a Christmas conference call. Or begin an Advent tradition like the family who asked all of the scattered relatives to purchase an Advent candle wreath. They simply coordinated their schedules according to the various time zones so all of them could light their candles each week at exactly the same moment.

Try to save up for a visit next year. One scattered family sets aside a small sum of money each month. Each nuclear family sends the money to a designated "treasurer," who saves it for the following Christmas so everyone can travel to a different home each holiday. This is great way to ensure not only extended family memories but also that the same family doesn't end up with the cranberry sauce on their carpet every year!

Remember to pray. Even though you're not able to get together with all the family members at Christmas, don't forget to pray for each other—and for a good holiday season for everyone.

Although I've spent the last six Christmas seasons working, I still love the holidays—their colors, sights, sounds, nostalgia. My husband, Jack, and I like to sit in the dark, look at the tree lights, and listen to the beautifully simple carol, . . . O Holy Night.

Last Christmas, Jack and I were with his family. This year, we'll be with my family: my mom; dad; brother, Oren; and sisters, Starla and Angela. The Paris family loves to celebrate, and the holidays are no exception. Christmas morning we meet in our pajamas or sweats at Mom and Dad's house. After we empty our stockings, my dad— the current patriarch of the family—reads the Christmas story; then we sing carols and worship together.

Two years ago, my folks had just moved from our childhood home to another house the week before Christmas, so we celebrated early. After opening gifts, we went to the old house. As we sat on the floor, bundled up in our coats because the heat was off, we shared funny stories and spiritual landmarks that had happened in that house. We prayed, thanking God for all the wonderful memories. Then we went to the new house and dedicated it to God.

My sister Starla also got engaged that day. When I tried to sing the song I'd written for her, we all cried. It was an incredibly emotional day. We really missed my family the year and a half we moved from Arkansas to live in Nashville.

TWILA PARIS

'Tis the Season of Sibling Stress

JAN SILVIOUS

"My older brother doesn't like us to talk about spiritual matters, so we all have to be careful around him."

"My middle sister has constant marital problems and belittles her children. . . . Things never change."

"I have trouble getting along with my younger sister because she constantly criticizes my clothes, job, boyfriend, you name it."

We women like to cling to an alluring holiday idea: Home is always warm and inviting, decorated with fond childhood memories, adorned with a love that continues uninterrupted by parental discord or sibling conflict.

For many women, that ideal is true. The holidays *do* live up to our expectation of family closeness. But for many others, the annual trek homeward and Thanksgiving or Christmas are often fraught with tensions like those echoed above. When the camaraderie is there, old patterns of relating can cause spoken or unspoken stresses if they're not acknowledged and constructively dealt with.

Take the Matthews family, for example. Year after year, when the family gathers for the holidays, the same sister takes charge, the same brother sees to the details, the same sister comes late, the same recipes are consumed while surface conversation is lightly passed back and forth. No one mentions the secret transgressions everyone knows about. No one asks about the missing mate who has been divorced out of the family. No one speaks of painful childhood memories. No one brings up topics that might stir up strife. For the Matthewses, denial and avoidance are the highly developed coping skills of the season. After the brothers and sisters embrace and return to their separate lives, the events of the season are filed away under *T* for trivia. But somehow, that "sibling connection" has been maintained.

Stress Is Inevitable during the Holidays

When I recently asked fifty women of varying ages, educational backgrounds, and spiritual maturity levels whether or not they looked forward to the holidays, they overwhelmingly responded yes. But when I asked them if there was one brother or sister who created tension, the majority quickly named one particular person.

Interestingly enough, these same women, when asked how their parents felt when all the brothers and sisters came home, responded positively. When quizzed about how they cope with inevitable sibling strain, they were vague and conciliatory:

"We usually just change the subject or laugh and say, 'OK, let's avoid a fight here.'"

"I pray, talk with my husband, and sometimes cry."

"I take a deep breath and ask God to help me forgive."

"I just block it out."

"I get angry but don't show it."

"We avoid talking about anything that will be upsetting."

Is It Time for a Turnaround in Your Family?

If you are sufficiently dissatisfied with the status quo of your adult sibling relationships, there *is* hope for improvement. It requires risking rejection. It also requires a willingness to change.

Often the kind of relational turnaround that brings lasting, satisfying results is an exercise in three steps forward, two steps back. But with persistence, consistency,

and maturity, you eventually will witness change. Here are some steps you can take to work toward improving your sibling connections.

If you really desire a change, examine yourself first. You must be willing to deal with "the plank in your own eye" before you remove the "speck of sawdust in your brother's eye."

Make sure you objectively scrutinize your own behavior for anything that could hurt your sister or brother. Are you domineering under the guise of being "motherly"? Are you condescending because she is your younger sister? Do you criticize your brother because he is the wild-and-crazy, unconventional family embarrassment? Do you view him as a pain? All of these reactions are counterproductive to a healthy relationship. Until you have confessed your wrong attitude to God and to your sibling, there is no room for conversation. You will be shut out and resented until you are willing to humble yourself, acknowledge your own wrong behavior, and accept your responsibility to change.

Prepare yourself to be with your siblings. "My oldest sister always seemed to get most of our parents' praise," admits Jodie. "It's hard not to feel resentful when she lords it over the rest of us. I feel like snipping back." Recognize that your hot-button is sensitive—particularly at the holidays. Decide what your response will be when you know you'll be around that irritating sibling. If you're caught off guard and allow your anger to explode, you will be the loser. If you really want a healthy relationship with your sibling, remember the scriptural admonition, "Everyone should be quick to listen, slow to speak and slow to become angry, for man's anger does not bring about the righteous life that God desires" (James 1:19-20).

Take your sister or brother seriously. "I still tend to treat my younger brother like the goofy, irresponsible kid he used to be," says Linda. "But in reality he's married, has kids, and is doing well in his career." Neither of you is a child, and you both deserve the respect adults give one another. Even if your sibling refuses to acknowledge your adulthood, "Do to others as you would have them do to you." If you are adamant about change, it must begin with you, no matter how anyone else responds.

Express a genuine interest in your brother's or sister's family. "My brother's wife is a problem because of her chronic sarcasm," Tina confesses. "If she's not happy, no one's happy." Admittedly, some family members are more difficult than others to

care about. But make an effort to get to know each one as a very special person. Talk with your in-laws and your nieces and nephews about their lives. Approach those moments as times when you can encourage. This genuine interest could go miles toward opening the door to a brother's or sister's heart. Even if he or she rejects your interest, your sibling will appreciate whatever you do for his or her children.

Communicate with one another. Most families are either bound by silence or energized by arguments. Neither qualifies as true communication. Take time during the holidays to listen to what is being said, as well as to express your own view. If you need to hammer out a long-standing conflict, find a private time and place to have your conversation.

Recognize that you can control what happens in the situation. Remember, you can limit the time you spend with your brother or sister. You also can pray for your sibling. This is a powerful investment in his or her life. God's ways are not our ways, but his ways are wonderful, so to pray confidently for the very best in your brother's or sister's life is a gift you can give with pleasure.

Finally, the Scriptures give us a picture of how brothers and sisters in Christ are to relate to one another—and the same truths apply to brothers and sisters in the flesh: "Therefore, as God's chosen people, holy and dearly loved, clothe yourselves with compassion, kindness, humility, gentleness and patience. Bear with each other and forgive whatever grievances you may have against one another. Forgive as the Lord forgave you" (Col. 3:12-13).

Changes in your sibling connections require changes in your life. If you view the process as an adventure in discovering God's best, you won't be defeated by setbacks and rejections. Once you have committed yourself to a plan for change that honors God and gives respect to your sibling—as well as to yourself—you will discover new strength and deeper insights in your journey toward maturity.

"Hey, quit complaining. I've matched you shovelful for shovelful all morning."

We Have Different Views of the Holidays

Dr. Diane Mandt Langberg

Question: *My husband and I have very different views about the holidays. I like to pull out all the stops and decorate our home from top to bottom. My husband thinks it's a waste of money. I buy meaningful, romantic presents, but he's unimaginative in the gift-giving department. I'm constantly disappointed during this time of year, and it's causing tension in our marriage.*

Answer: Several years ago, I counseled a couple with a similar problem. The husband grew up in a home that had very few traditions. Birthdays were ignored, Mother's Day never happened, and Christmas was quite barren. When the holidays approached, this man felt totally inadequate. He admitted feeling as if he needed to follow a set of rules that no one had ever taught him. Could this be the case with *your* husband?

Another possibility is that your husband grew up unused to the beauty of "unnecessary" things in his life—flowers or small presents given "just because." Perhaps his family never nurtured his romantic side. Whatever the reason, it's important to stop battling over whose way is right at Christmas.

Marriage brings together two different lives and traditions. The result should be unique. Whether it's in the way you raise your children or the way you celebrate Christmas, what you do as a couple should be a combination of you both.

Philippians 2:3 says, "Do nothing out of selfish ambition . . . but in humility consider others better than yourselves." First, look at your own heart. If you're not willing to let go of your way of doing things, you will always be at odds with your husband. Instead, ask him what he thinks is important about Christmas. What did he like or dislike about how *his* family celebrated? What makes him uncomfortable about the way you are used to celebrating Christmas? And what does he *like* about it? The answers to these questions will help you understand who your husband is and what is important to him.

If he is uncomfortable with the idea of traditions in general, remind your husband that God repeatedly used tradition in Scripture—for example, the Passover and the Lord's Supper—to remind us of certain truths and to draw us closer to him. Family traditions can serve the same purpose. Then ask him if he'll pray with you about how the two of you can establish a home that celebrates Christmas in a way that lifts up Christ and reflects your family's uniqueness.

This change in your approach to the holidays will require lots of open communication, effort, and willingness to let go of "your" way of celebrating. It is my prayer that in future years, your home will celebrate Christmas in a way that honors the birth of Jesus, first and foremost, and reflects two unique individuals in a new way.

Traditions WITH A TWIST

Last Christmas, our extended family started a new tradition—we rented a cabin at a Christian camp. Since it was the off season, we had the camp to ourselves.

My entire family took a walk in the woods and gathered items to decorate a small tree. Then all the adults created a treasure hunt for the children. In the evening, we walked to the outdoor worship center using flashlights to guide our way. There we sang Christmas carols and set up our Nativity scene on the altar, which was spotlighted. Then Grandpa shut off the lights, and we were in total darkness in the quiet woods, under the moon and the stars, with God and each other.

Later we returned to the cottage to exchange gifts. The children shared their treasures and did craft projects. It was a Christmas to remember—complete with hot chocolate, cookies, a cozy fire, and a sense of family.

PAULA R. EWART

I Didn't Want to Share My Mom

MAYO MATHERS

I still remember that first Thanksgiving, seventeen of us crowded around the bountiful table, knees touching, elbows bumping. My stomach was already in knots—and the afternoon had just begun.

"Shall we pray?" My stepfather, Don, beamed down the table at this group of acquaintances transformed into relatives by his marriage to my mother. He stretched his arms out, signaling us to hold hands.

"We're going to pray," I whispered to Tyler, my then two-year-old son. "Hold Aunt Donita's hand."

Don's teenage daughter grimaced as she held out a reluctant finger for Tyler's eager grasp. He immediately pulled her hand to his mouth and clamped his teeth around her finger. Donita gasped as I finally pried her finger free, and then she proclaimed vehemently, "I am *never* having kids!"

Don smiled benignly and began his prayer. "Our Father, we thank Thee for this food and this family. . . ." *He's the only one thankful,* I thought to myself.

At first, I'd been thrilled when Mom married Don fifteen years ago. Widowed at thirty-two, she'd committed her life to raising my brother, sister, and me. But all us kids were married by then, with families of our own, and I was glad she wouldn't be alone anymore.

Don understood the pain of losing a spouse. His wife had died several years earlier, leaving him with three teenage daughters. When Mom and Don announced their plans to marry, both families rejoiced, and at the wedding, all six kids stood up with the bride and groom. It couldn't have been more perfect.

But when Mom said "I do," it brought drastic changes. My brother, sister, and I had been the center of her world. Even as an adult, I drew tremendous strength from this knowledge. Before her marriage to Don, Mom frequently drove the more than three hours to my house. Once my kids were asleep, we'd brew a pot of tea and curl up for homey late-night chats.

Her marriage changed that. Secure in her relationship with her own children, she concentrated on her relationship with Don and his family. Understanding this didn't make it any easier.

The first time I visited Mom and Don after their wedding, reality set in. Mom had sold her house and moved to Don's dairy farm. Gone was the furniture I'd grown up with, the curios our family had collected, the dishes I'd argued with my sister over washing.

The photographs on the wall were of people I didn't know, occasions I hadn't participated in. For the first time, it occurred to me I'd never be able to go "home" again. That place of my heart no longer existed.

The responsibilities of the dairy farm made it impossible for Mom to get away to visit me. And when I went to see her, cozy visiting was just as impossible. Shouting interesting bits of news at her as we fed fifty bawling calves just wasn't the same.

I began to feel orphaned, and Don was the easiest person to blame. I was thirty-five years old and wanted to throw a three-year-old's tantrum. I envisioned myself grabbing Don by the throat and screaming, "I want my mother *back!*"

"God," I wept into my pillow after one particularly difficult visit, "I miss my mother! Will things ever be the same again?"

Would you prefer she be alone, just so she can be at your beck and call? God countered.

No, I never wished her back to widowhood. But my negative feelings had caught me off guard. I'd expected only minor adjustments with this remarriage since my brother, sister, and I were settled into our own lives, as were Don's children. But the collective relatives were seldom together long enough to feel like a family.

Then one weekend after Mom and Don had been married a few years, the kids and I went home for a visit. That was the weekend Don's daughter Deanna brought home her boyfriend, George. After dinner, the adults sat in the living room talking. For the first time, I felt that longed-for sense of belonging. When I finally glanced down at my watch, I gasped. "It's nearly midnight!" I hated to leave the comfy setting, but I had a long drive home the next day. Reluctantly, I excused myself and went to bed.

Snug under a mound of blankets, I listened to laughter drifting up the stairs. *What was I missing?* I considered rejoining the fun, but instead I nestled deeper into the warm bed, feeling very much at home in the old farmhouse.

That is, until breakfast the next morning, when I discovered the reason for their laughter. Deanna and George had announced their engagement. I must have registered appropriate shock because everyone laughed again.

"We didn't think you were ever going to go to bed," Deanna laughed, "and we wanted to tell Dad the news alone."

All my good feelings about the previous night vanished. I felt like an intruder in my mother's home, and a dawdling one at that!

After congratulating them, I made a hasty retreat upstairs to pack. Fighting humiliated tears, I stuffed my clothes into the suitcase and said my good-byes. *How could I have felt like this was beginning to be my home, my family?*

Before I even reached the highway, however, reason returned. If I had been announcing my engagement, wouldn't I have wanted a little privacy? If I were struggling with my enlarged family, it made sense my stepsister was, too.

As time passed, Mom began adding her own personal touches to the farmhouse. Each time I visited, something familiar from my childhood had found its way into the decor. The lumpy clay pitcher formed by my ten-year-old hands now sat on the kitchen shelf. The wooden bowl carved by my brother was displayed on the coffee table, and my sister's hand-sewn comforter covered the bed in the guest room.

I was especially happy when Mom repapered the kitchen. The room had been decorated around the garish orange and green of the sixties, and I loved the softer color scheme Mom chose.

Don's daughters, however, weren't as enthusiastic about the new kitchen when they came home to visit. At first I didn't understand their reaction and felt they weren't giving Mom a fair chance. But as I prayed about this, God helped me see these changes through my stepsisters' eyes.

I realized as Mom put out familiar objects from our family, some from their family disappeared. The kitchen I thought looked so pretty now had been lovingly decorated by their mother. To them it must have felt as if her personality had been ripped from the room along with the yellowed paper.

Although every change Mom made in the farmhouse made it feel more familiar, one Christmas my brother, sister, and I discussed the possibility of having Christmas at one of our homes instead of at the farm, where the dinner and gift exchange had to be squeezed in among endless chores.

Astoundingly, the suggestion met with loud protests from all our children. "It won't be like Christmas if we're not at the farm!" cried my niece Katie.

"What about the sleigh bells?" asked my son, Tyler. "How will we know when to hide without them?" He referred to our tradition of ringing sleigh bells, signaling Santa's arrival and time for all the children to run upstairs and hide while he unloaded his sleigh.

As I listened to their complaints, one thing became very clear. The farm might not feel like home to me, but it was home to the grandkids. This was the only house they could remember Grandma living in, and it was as much a part of their heritage as our grandmother's house was to us.

That realization—more than anything else—made the line between our family and Don's family soften in my eyes. Knowing my children saw everyone simply as their family made all the difference.

The greatest proof of all came last Thanksgiving. Once again the two families were crowded around a bountiful table, knees touching, elbows bumping—but there were no longer knots in my stomach. And as usual, Don signaled for us to hold hands as we prayed. Tyler, now a teenager, sat calmly. However, two-year-old Levi, son of my stepsister Danise, soon wearied of his grandpa's prayer. I could sense Danise's growing tension. How well I remembered the days of having the only toddler at the table!

Just as Don brought his prayer to an end, Levi banged his fork loudly against his plate, startling Tyler with the noise. As Levi laughed in delight, Tyler looked at me and grinned. "I'm never having kids!" he stated.

I laughed, remembering when those same words were spoken in response to him, and looked at the faces circling the table. When Mom married Don, time didn't stop for me to adjust to the changes. It kept moving forward, and I had the choice to move with it or be dragged along in the dust. Even though I'd spent much of that time digging my heels firmly into the past, a miracle had been unfolding. All the while, the people gathered around this table were being transformed from acquaintances to relatives to family. My family.

My Best Childhood Christmas

_____

_____

_____

_____

_____

_____

_____

_____

_____

_____

_____

_____

_____

_____

_____

_____

_____

_____

_____

_____

_____

_____

_____

_____

Favorite Holiday Memories

Happy Season's Eatings!

Oh, those delectable Christmas smells and tastes that encourage us all to eat too much: Grandma's stuffing, fresh cranberries, the wafting of fresh-baked turkey and pumpkin pie. But in spite of our increased waistlines, we all agree—it wouldn't be Christmas without at least *some* of our favorite traditional foods. And as we eat together with family and friends, we enjoy the rewards of renewed companionship—an earthly taste of heaven.

My favorite memory of Christmas is making homemade cranberry relish by grinding up oranges, apples, and fresh cranberries. I loved it because it took forever to make it, and everybody in the family had a part.

SUSAN ASHTON

Traditions WITH A TWIST

Our six-year-old son, Mickey, loves animals. Last year he suggested our family trek up into the mountains near our home to decorate a tree with edible ornaments so that the wild animals could have their own Christmas feast. We strung popcorn and cranberries for garlands, covered pinecones with peanut butter and birdseed for ornaments, made "Christmas bulbs" out of whole mandarin oranges, and completed our decorations with dried ears of corn, apples, and carrots.

On Christmas Day, after hiking through waist-high snow, we found "the perfect tree." Once it was decorated, we hid and waited for our animal friends to discover our surprise. The sight of our son's eyes lighting up when a few birds and a squirrel came and nibbled on our tree will forever glow in our memories. From now on, each Christmas will be filled with warm, loving mountain memories.

DENISE NELSON

"I'm not leaving you any more milk and cookies 'til you've lost a few pounds."

My father always had to work on the holiday, so we celebrated most of my childhood Christmas mornings without him. He was a closet gourmet cook and especially loved to bake extravagant breads and other sweets during the winter holidays. So on Christmas morning there would be some treat already baked and ready for us. There were breads drizzled with frosting to be toasted under the broiler or pull-apart orange marmalade rolls for warming. All of them were tasty, full of candied fruit, and braided or molded. Each was decorated with the perfection of a blue-collar worker who had always been an artist inside.

Vinita Hampton Wright

Traditions WITH A TWIST

When I hosted a holiday dinner for friends several years ago, I surprised my guests with some "sweet symbolism" at their dinner plates. I printed the following poem from an unknown writer on a piece of Christmas stationery:

> *A significant symbol of Christmas*
> *Is the simple cane.*
> *Its shape is the crook of a shepherd—*
> *One of the first who came.*
>
> *The lively peppermint flavor*
> *Is the regal gift of spice.*
> *The white is Jesus' purity,*
> *The red, his sacrifice.*
>
> *The narrow stripes are friendship*
> *And the nearness of his love.*
>
> *Eternal, sweet compassion,*
> *A gift from God above.*
>
> *The candy cane reminds us all*
> *Of just how much God cared.*
> *And like his Christmas gift to us,*
> *It's meant to be broken and shared.*
> *Merry Christmas!*

Then I wrapped the stationery around a candy cane and tied the package with a red ribbon. The "sweet symbolism" added meaning to an otherwise hectic season. It was such a hit that I've made it part of my holiday dinner celebrations ever since.

CHERYL DOLLAS

My Favorite Recipe

For extra zip to your holiday menu, make your favorite stuffing recipe. Then add stuffed, sliced green olives. The olive green and pimento red will provide a dash of color in an otherwise traditional dish.

Barbara Finstrom Calvert

JAM SESSION

One Sunday evening, I overheard my five-year-old daughter, Julie, practicing "Hark! the Herald Angels Sing," a song she'd been rehearsing that morning in church for next week's Christmas program. It was all I could do to suppress my laughter when, in place of "with angelic host proclaim," Julie sang, "with the jelly toast proclaim."

MARILYN CLARK

Traditions WITH A TWIST

Two weeks before Christmas, my mom, my sister, and I set a "baking date." We get together on a Saturday at one of our houses and bake a variety of cookie favorites. Flour, conversation, and laughter fly around the kitchen.

Our husbands spend the day together, too: They go Christmas shopping, eat out, and enjoy an early movie or bowling.

Then in the evening, all of us—men and women—gather together for spiced cider and cookie samplings in the family room. By the end of that day, we have all sorts of goodies to share with each other—and to give away for inexpensive gifts. It's a great way to reduce the stress of Christmas baking *and* enjoy quality family time.

MONA ACKELSON

"Nancy broke last year's record—30 dozen Christmas cookies and 12 fruitcakes."

My Favorite Recipe

For our family, Christmas just wouldn't be Christmas without the traditional making of our favorite bonbons:

1 cup chunky peanut butter
1 cup confectioners' sugar
10 maraschino cherries, chopped fine

Mix together well, and make into small balls. Chill in freezer until hard. Melt a small package of chocolate chips (6 ounces) and $\frac{1}{4}$ pound of paraffin wax in the top of a double boiler, with water underneath so the mixture won't scorch (mixture should never boil). Using tongs, dip the balls one at a time in the chocolate. Set to cool on waxed paper until completely dry.

These bonbons are so yummy they won't last long at your house. And they're perfect for gift giving, too, in a pretty container.

Josie Cramer

Lighten Up

DRS. SHARON AND DAVID SNEED

"Every December, I gain ten pounds! Then I have to diet like crazy to take it off each spring," my friend Ellen recently complained.

If you're caught on this holiday weight-gain roller coaster, take note. An increase of only 200 extra calories per day (a few Christmas cookies or a handful of nuts) can cause you to gain at least five pounds by the end of the holiday season. Most holiday foods are high in sugar and fat—the very constituents that make us gain body fat.

But the good news is, the following strategies will keep you from gaining weight over the holidays and having to diet this spring.

Party Hints

Here's what you can do to cut calories, whether you're invited to a church cookie exchange or the company Christmas party.

Never go to a party hungry. Have a high-protein snack before you leave, such as a glass of milk, cottage cheese, or a small sandwich. Don't justify overconsumption by starving yourself beforehand.

Plan ahead. What kinds of foods will be served at this party? Before you get there, try to set a mental limit of how much you will eat.

Be aware of fats and calories. Many cooks pull out the stops at holiday time. The result usually is a smorgasbord of high-fat items. Be especially wary of cream cheese, sour cream, mayonnaise, nuts, high-calorie punch or juices, chips, sausage, pastries, cookies, greasy crackers, cheese, cakes, pies, and certain candies. Would you rather eat one cup of strawberries or its caloric equivalent, two macadamia nuts?

Size up the buffet. Before you fill your plate, note all choices available, then go back, fill your plate *once* with foods from all food groups, and go easy on the high-fat items.

Distance yourself from the food table. Once you've served yourself, stand at the other end of the room away from the food. Try not to mill around the buffet table with others who are picking up everything in sight—you'll only feel tempted to do the same. And when your plate or napkin is empty, throw it away so you're not tempted to go back for seconds.

Be sociable. Go to a party to be with the people. The more you talk, the less time you have for eating.

Drink lots of noncaloric liquids. Keep a glass of mineral water with a twist of lemon in your hand at all times. Refill it often. Also, hot liquids such as coffee and tea can help quench hunger pains.

Company's Coming

What you can do when your guests expect traditional holiday fare.

Don't buy too far in advance. Don't feel compelled to buy several bags of holiday candy on December 1 if your party is two weeks away. If you must serve these items, purchase them the day of the party and vow not to open them until guests arrive.

Prepare low-calorie foods. Include the standard vegetable dips, but also incorporate low-calorie selections such as cottage cheese or yogurt dip into your menu. Try small chicken, beef, or vegetable kabobs cooked on an inside grill. Assorted fruit kabobs are also nice. Consult a cookbook for other low-calorie party food ideas.

Give foods a great presentation. Appearance is half the game in cooking, so become an expert on garnish. Make an attractive arrangement out of cut vegetables in a basket lined with fresh lettuce leaves. Arrange fruit kabobs on toothpicks stuck into a halved eggplant, shiny side up. Use fresh herbs to accentuate the fact that your foods are flavorful and innovative.

Enable guests to control their portion sizes. Anything may be eaten in small amounts—even chocolate! Cut desserts into small portions. This gives guests the freedom to take small servings—or seconds if they wish.

Give away the extras. If you receive high-calorie food gifts or have leftovers that are too tempting to resist, give these items away or send them home with guests.

Home Is Where the Calories Are

Our kitchen can be our own worst enemy in the battle of the bulge. Here are some tips to win the war on the home front.

Resist the urge to bake if you can't say no to sweets. More women gain weight from their own good deeds than from any other holiday nutrition problem! Do the people you are baking for really need all those extra calories? Homemade gifts such as jams, jellies, barbecue sauces, marinades, healthful breads, ornaments, and plants are just as meaningful. Keep this in mind if you know you will eat half the Christmas cookies you bake.

Don't set out foods as decoration. Coffee-table bowls of holiday nuts or colorful Christmas candies may make your home look like a magazine photo, but they are an open invitation to snack on handfuls of fat and sugar.

Develop a portfolio of good-for-you Christmas recipes. Bookstores offer a variety of health-conscious cookbooks that provide excellent recipes for family favorites such as hot wassail, almond bread, and apple pancakes. Healthy foods often taste better and fresher than high-fat alternatives.

Take the holiday focus off food. Use other special memory makers, such as crafts and family activities, to make this holiday special.

"My wife is dieting. Would you have anything like chocolate-covered celery?"

Traditions WITH A TWIST

Every Christmas morning, my siblings and I would awaken to the smells of Mom's fresh-baked candlebraid bread (our Norwegian neighbors called it Santa Lucia Crown). Each year the youngest child in the family got to light the three red candles nestled in the bread and then carry it from room to room (sometimes with Mom's help), letting its smell and a cheery "Merry Christmas!" wake up the other members of the family. When all were dressed, we would have a simple breakfast picnic of candlebraid bread and juice on the floor on a Christmas quilt made by my grandmother.

RAY CARMEN

"Do I have to give thanks for all the vegetables or just the pumpkin pie?"

Christmas Cautions

DR. PAUL REISSER

The following popular Christmas plants are potentially hazardous for little children's mouths and stomachs (and pets' too!):

Poinsettias. This plant is considered minimally toxic. Its leaves, when chewed, can cause irritation of the mouth and throat and occasionally nausea and vomiting.

Mistletoe. If your child swallows more than three mistletoe leaves or berries, call your nearest hospital emergency room or poison hot line as soon as possible and follow their directions. Ingestion can cause vomiting, diarrhea, seizures, and serious changes in blood pressure.

Holly. In addition to holly's finger-pricking potential, it can be quite toxic. Eating one or two berries can cause the following symptoms: nausea, vomiting, abdominal pain, drowsiness, and stupor. Seek medical advice immediately.

Make this year's Christmas more anxiety-free by placing such items out of reach of little ones.

My Favorite Recipe

Mix your favorite brownies, as directed on box or in recipe. Place paper cupcake cups (a Christmas pattern is nice for the holidays) in muffin tins. Fill tins half full with the brownie mixture. Unwrap miniature Reese's peanut butter cups, and place in the middle of each muffin cup. Press down until even with the level of the brownie mix. Bake as directed in recipe or on box. These treats are great for kids' parties or lunchboxes.

Evangeline F. Schock

Traditions

Making Christmas cookies with my mother is one of my favorite childhood memories. But as a single career woman, I simply don't have time to make the abundant assortment my mom used to make. Instead, I settled on one favorite cut-out ginger cookie recipe as my special holiday cookie, and I use a different shape to cut them out each year. Making them has become my own little tradition. I set aside a baking day early in December, and the familiar smells of cinnamon, ginger, and molasses never fail to put me in the Christmas spirit. My friends have come to expect a bag of my cookies each year—so it simplifies my gift giving as well!

JAN SENN

Calories Don't Count When . . .

Elizabeth Cody Newenhuyse

The holidays are coming: Thanksgiving, when we gather together to ask the Lord's blessing—and eat stuffing, soaked in butter. Christmas, season of the Savior's birth—and the neighborhood cookie exchange.

Should we resign ourselves to the annual bloat? No. There's good news—I've discovered that the body doesn't utilize all calories in the same way. In fact, according to my exhaustive research, calories don't count when . . .

They're eaten while standing. This applies equally to licking batter from the bowl, snitching miniature meatballs from the hors d'oeuvre platter, and eating ice cream out of the carton.

They're eaten at the mall. The energy exerted in trekking around a mall is equivalent to a hard session of step aerobics—plus there's a lot more to look at. Therefore, a sticky-bun break is entirely acceptable. It is to the shopper what Gatorade is to the athlete.

They're consumed late in the evening. You may be struggling to assemble a Barbie village on Christmas Eve. Suddenly, you crave caramel corn. That's a signal your body needs a sugar lift. Calories ingested after nine o'clock are used to maintain alertness, not fat cells.

You are (a) premenstrual, (b) overdrawn on your checking account, (c) the victim of an unfortunate haircut. These are "comfort calories," and you *deserve* them.

They're served by your mother. Remember, your mother's chief joy in life is to see you content. When you eat, you brighten her day.

They're served in the spirit of Christian sisterhood. In some Third World countries, refusing the food your host offers is an insult of the gravest sort. Who would be so ill-mannered as to turn away a beribboned loaf of pumpkin bread? The body rewards such charity by immediately turning the calories into lean muscle tissue.

You follow a special palate-cleansing procedure. Say you eat a piece of homemade fudge. Afterward, simply chomp on a celery stick. This is similar to erasing a recording by taping over it. The body registers only the vegetable. Happy Season's Eatings!

Our Traditional Holiday Menu

Secret Family Recipes

_____

_____

_____

_____

_____

_____

_____

_____

_____

_____

_____

_____

_____

_____

_____

_____

_____

_____

_____

_____

_____

_____

_____

_____

_____

_____

_____

_____

Lo-Cal, Lo-Guilt Specialties

Hassle-Free Gifts That Are Worth Giving

Just the words *holiday shopping* are enough to cause stress in anyone's pre-Christmas life. If the hassle of finding that perfect gift leaves *you* feeling harassed this Christmas, maybe it's time for a change. Great gifts don't have to cost a lot—or even a penny. The key is not how much you spend but your attitude of love. As you enjoy the following gift ideas and stories, take time to thank God for the greatest gift of all: his Son, the reason we celebrate Christmas!

I love the holidays because traditionally our family slows down at Christmastime. We don't emphasize gift giving as much as creating a wonderful atmosphere in the home. Four out of the last six years, Gary, the kids, and I have gone skiing with the Grant side of the family. We don't even take gifts. We might buy little things—one year my sister gave me chocolate-covered potato chips—but basically, our gift is being together. There are twenty-five of us who usually go on that trip. We rent a big house, and it's wonderful!

AMY GRANT

Twenty-five Gifts You'll Love to Give—and They'll Love to Get!

HOLLY G. MILLER

Are you tired of giving predictable presents—those ties that blind, cookies that "settle" during shipment, electronic gadgets that supposedly streamline life but clutter closets? Why not consider the following list instead? Some gifts are homemade, others are tailor-made; they range in price from free to inexpensive. But they're all guaranteed to be ones your recipients will never forget!

For Teenagers Who Like to Do Their Own Thing

Treat them to an inexpensive night on the town. Buy a gift certificate for their favorite fast food (pizza? pasta? burgers?), then add a couple of movie passes. Top it off with coupons for an after-the-show treat at the local ice-cream shop.

For the College Student

Buy (or make) an oversized laundry bag and stencil his or her name on the front in bold letters. Fill the bag with bottles or boxes of detergent, fabric softener, and bleach. Include a roll of quarters for the washing machine and a couple of magazines to help the student pass the time while the jeans tumble dry.

For New Grandparents Who Live Out of State

Buy a small photo album and label it "A Day in the Life of . . ." (fill in the baby's name). Record on film all the events in Baby's typical day, such as taking a morning bubble bath, eating breakfast, walking in the park, playing, greeting Daddy after work, being rocked to sleep. Plan to replace the photos a couple of times a year as Baby becomes more active and his or her "day" is more eventful. Variation: Although not as portable (grandparents never leave home without their snapshots), a videotape with Baby as the star makes an animated alternative to this gift.

For the Office Gift Exchange

Make sure your coworker's coffee breaks at home are more leisurely than the ones you share at work. Choose a pretty mug with an appropriate message, then add a small bag of flavored coffee (or tea), a homemade coffee cake, and a devotional book.

For Your Children Who Have "Left the Nest"

Buy an address book and enter the names, phone numbers, addresses, birthdays, and anniversary dates of family and friends. The book will save you from sounding too motherly ("Don't forget to send Uncle Fred a card next Tuesday!") and help them assume responsibility for writing thank-you notes, building a Christmas-card file, compiling invitation lists, and remembering friends on special occasions.

For Young Parents

Offer to keep their children overnight once a month for a year. Arrange to pick up your young houseguests in midafternoon so Mom can relax as she prepares for her evening out (or in) with her favorite "date."

For the Nursing-Home Resident

Fill a large, covered candy dish with red and green hard candies for the holidays, and pledge to restock the goodies several times during the year (peppermint hearts for Valentine's Day, candy corn in October). Not only will the treats be appreciated by your elderly friend, but they also will become a drawing card for nurses and other residents to stop by his or her room, say hello, and sample the latest goody.

For Pet Lovers

Offer to care for Fido in their house or yours during their family's vacation. Boarding costs are high, and many pet owners bypass travel opportunities rather than put their pet in a kennel.

For Grandma from Her Teenaged Grandkids

Teens on a budget can delight Grandma by treating her to a monthly movie "date" at her place. Rent (or borrow from the library) a video everyone will enjoy, buy a six-pack of soft drinks, and don't leave home without the popcorn. Two tips: Strive for variety—one month a mystery, the next month a comedy, the following month a musical—and remember, cleanup duties are the responsibility of the giver.

For the Mom Who Homeschools

Show your support by scheduling a couple of visits to her "class" in the weeks leading up to Christmas. This will give the teaching mom time to slip away for some holiday shopping without shirking her duties. Build a lesson around your special talents and interests—music or art or computer science or literature—or plan a field trip to a nearby museum.

For Special Neighbors

Arrange for a delivery of firewood to be shared with your next-door neighbor. Announce the gift in a card tucked between several white birch logs wrapped with a wide taffeta ribbon. The logs make a lovely hearth decoration during the holidays and serve as a reminder of a gift as warm as your friendship. Tip: Stack the communal woodpile within a few steps of both properties.

For Older Readers

Introduce a favorite senior citizen to the wonders of books on tape. Perfect for persons who love to read but whose eyes are failing, the books are available to borrow from libraries at no charge. Announce the gift by buying and wrapping a small headset, tape recorder, and favorite inspirational book on tape. Plan to exchange the tapes regularly, or offer to take your friends to the library so they can select their own titles.

For the Young Kitty Owner

If parents have said yes to the idea of a Christmas kitten for their child, plan to supply the necessary extras. Gift-wrap a plastic dishpan with a sack of litter, kitty-box liners, catnip toy, and tiny collar.

For Someone Who Doesn't Drive

Give the gift of time. Set aside two hours a week to serve as chauffeur, escort, or errand runner for a special person who may no longer drive a car. Among the typical stops: the library, grocery, pharmacy, beauty shop, post office.

For Your Parents

Gather the family's old home movies—vintage films of holiday celebrations, birthday parties, family vacations—and have them transferred to a single videotape at a local camera shop. Depending on your budget, you can add an introduction, title, narration, and background music. Popping a tape into a VCR is a lot easier than setting up a projector and screen. Just think of the fun you'll have viewing it after Christmas dinner!

For a Student's Final-Exam Week

Since final-exam week is the last campus activity before the holiday break, arrange to send a "Final-Exam Survival Kit" as an early Christmas gift. Include healthy alternatives to vending-machine snacks: fresh fruit, raisins, homemade trail mix, granola, cheese, and cans of juice. Then top it off with a triple batch of every dorm's favorite—chocolate-chip cookies!

For the Young Mother

Pamper her with an appointment for a "makeover"—haircut, manicure, facial. Let her choose the day, then volunteer to take care of the kids.

For the New Bride

Choose a favorite family dessert recipe, jot down the instructions on a recipe card, buy the appropriate baking pan, and arrange the required ingredients in the pan.

Wrap the pan and its contents in plastic and tie with a bright ribbon.

For Someone Who Is Housebound

Fill a pretty box with a selection of greeting cards appropriate for every occasion. Include cards for birthdays (all ages), anniversaries, sympathy, "thinking of you," graduation, and get-well greetings. Tuck in a roll of postage stamps and an ink pen.

For the Environmentally Conscious

Make (or buy) a wooden birdhouse. Add sandpaper, paint, stain, or other finishing materials. Don't forget to include an ample supply of birdseed and suet.

For the Blueberry Lover

Fill a light-blue basket with a variety of blueberry products such as a jar of homemade jam, muffin and pancake mix, syrup, a blueberry-scented candle, bath salts, room freshener, and light blue notepaper. The same "basket" idea works equally well when the theme is strawberry, lavender, peppermint, or other "flavors."

For the Preteen Girl

Make a drawstring pouch out of pretty chintz fabric and velvet ribbon. Fill the bag with toiletries suitable for an emerging young woman: light floral scent, natural lip gloss, clear nail polish, bubble bath, and dusting powder.

For Kids of All Ages

Create a "book of the month" club similar to the adult version. Send your recipients a different book each month, or allow them to choose from a few you've selected. Make sure to include inspirational books children might not see in their school libraries. This is a great way to encourage children to read and, at the same time, introduce them to Christian authors and themes.

For the Next Generation

Too often family members wait until death before their heirlooms are passed on to the next generation. Why not start the tradition of passing down a piece of family crystal, china, or silver each Christmas? Plan to tell the story behind the piece when it's unwrapped. Then encourage younger family members to display, use, and enjoy their treasures.

For a Friend Who Works Long Hours

Create a stack of "gift certificates" to be redeemed for one casserole a month for a year. The lucky recipient can specify days that promise to be particularly hectic and let you know a week in advance of the preferred "delivery." Shortly after the friend arrives home on the selected evening, dinner will appear at the door piping hot and ready to eat.

Hugs Given Here

As a middle-school teacher, I've found some subtle yet meaningful
ways to share my faith not only at Christmas but also year-round.

On my desk sits a photo of my family—my dear husband of thirty-two
years, our four great kids, and their spouses. When students ask to see
my picture, I always tell them that these people are God's gift to me.
I've found that multiparent kids are most touched by the picture—
and many often need my love and attention.

Behind my desk hangs a wreath with school-type ornaments on it
(glue, scissor, etc.) and a little slate that says Hugs Given Here.
This was a Christmas gift from our eldest daughter, but it now hangs
year-round because one day I looked up to see three sixth graders
standing quietly in line under the wreath. I was delighted to administer
those hugs—and many more since then! Though I'm in the classroom
to teach math, I feel my time would be spent in vain if I didn't also
teach sincerity, honesty, kindness, and—most of all—love.

MARION BURLESON

VIEWPOINTS

How Much Is Enough?

When it comes to material things, how do you determine how much is enough?
Here's what seven women had to say.

"A while ago I determined enough was enough when I discovered I'd go shopping for entertainment instead of need. Now, when I go shopping, I evaluate what I'm purchasing: Is it a necessity, or could my money be used for a more valuable purpose such as to feed the hungry or clothe the poor?" *JODY HILL*

"For three years I longed for our home to be built. I became grumpy and impatient while we lived in our summer cottage. Recently, tests revealed I have a life-threatening disease—cancer. Suddenly, I realize I have far too much. 'Enough' now seems to be the bare necessities." *GRETA DAWSON*

"God wants us to be able to help those in need. If we are always trying to get more material things, we can end up in debt. And if we are in debt, we may miss the opportunity to help someone who comes to us in need. I look to Philippians 4:4-13 and Luke 12:22-34 to help me be content in every situation and to know when enough is enough." *CHERYL DAVIS*

"My guideline to determine how much is enough is Proverbs 30:9: 'Lest I be full, and deny thee, and say, Who is the Lord? or lest I be poor, and steal, and take the name of my God in vain' (KJV). I hope to have enough so I don't have to dwell on my needs, but not so much that it calls attention to another's lack." *SUSAN PHILLIPS*

"As far as material things go, I try not to get too preoccupied with them. As the Gospels of Matthew and Luke tell us, we need to store up our riches in heaven, not on earth. *Enough* is when we start losing sight of the Lord's plan for our lives—to live with him forever in his kingdom." *NEVA M. ZIEGLER*

"I don't believe in a prosperity theology. Just because we have the means to purchase something doesn't mean God wants us to go ahead and buy it. Part of the call of the gospel is simplicity. If we lead a simple life, we'll be surprised at how little can be enough." *SUE GARRY*

"For me, I have enough when I can pay my mortgage and utilities on time; provide three average meals a day; have traditional and durable clothing; and have money to provide for the church, medical bills, and recreation." *KATHLEEN BELL*

Traditions WITH A TWIST

One of the special joys of our holiday season is "elving." Each year my husband and I select a different family we know, and for five to seven nights prior to Christmas, we leave "elf" gifts on their doorstep. The first night's gift is a special Christmas story for the children—which explains the spiritual significance of the colors and trimmings of the holiday.

The following nights' gifts might be homemade cookies or a Christmas ornament. Each gift is in a bag with a note from "the elves." On the final night of "elving," we reveal our identity. It's been heartwarming to see several of the families we've "elved" in previous years now elving someone they know.

Contributed by
BONNIE C. MARRET

"It's not fair . . . just 'cause you're a girl. . . ."

The Wish List

ELIZABETH MITTELSTAEDT

What a contrast my Christmases as an adult have been to the ones I experienced as a child! While my husband, Ditmar, was studying for his master's degree in Chicago, we enjoyed each holiday season with its festive store windows, twinkling lights, parties, and gifts—lots of them!

But as a young girl in communist Yugoslavia, my family celebrated the holidays simply. On Christmas Eve, we'd sit around the old farmhouse as my grandpa read the Christmas story. My only present was a large orange that I'd keep for days before savoring its sweet, juicy taste.

So when Ditmar's studies were over and we were appointed as career missionaries to Germany, I had mixed emotions. While I looked forward to telling my fellow Europeans about the true meaning of Christmas, I knew I'd miss the United States and the holiday traditions we'd begun.

I decided to make our last Christmas in Chicago extra special. I began decorating, baking, planning parties, and thinking about what to give Ditmar. I jotted down my wish list—a flannel nightgown, perfume, and a pair of brown gloves to match my coat—and planned to place it where Ditmar would be sure to find it.

But a few days later, before I could "plant" my list, Ditmar said, "Honey, you know we'll have a major cut in income on the mission field. Let's start now to prepare for the changes. This Christmas, let's exchange only one gift."

My heart sank, and sadness swept over me. My mind raced back to my childhood Christmases. *Will I be able to give up the things that make Christmas so special to me now?* I wondered.

We had a few friends over for a quiet Christmas Eve celebration, and when the last couple left, Ditmar said, "OK, honey, let's open our gifts."

Sure, one present, I thought. *Big deal.* Inside the box was a beautiful ivory sweater.

Then Ditmar handed me four more gifts. I was stunned and upset. "I thought we'd agreed on one!" I protested.

"These aren't from me," he said. "They're from a few friends at church."

I carefully unwrapped the biggest box. Nestled inside was a beautiful flannel nightgown trimmed with lace.

The next little package was tied with fancy ribbon. When I removed the gift wrap, I could read the box—*Eau de Parfum, Paris.*

The third present was a thin box from my favorite department store. In it were soft, brown leather gloves.

Suddenly, I remembered my list. My friends couldn't have seen it. Ditmar didn't even know about it. But God sees everything!

Then why a fourth package? I wondered. Nervously, I lifted the lid. Inside was an elegant silver dinner bell. *What do I need with a dinner bell on the mission field?* I thought, perplexed.

Suddenly, a Scripture came to mind: "For you know that it was not with perishable things such as silver or gold that you were redeemed . . . but with the precious blood of Christ" (1 Pet. 1:18-19).

Just then, a gentle whisper came to my heart: *Elizabeth, you're more valuable to me than silver and gold. You don't need to be afraid. Wherever you go, I'll take care of you. I know your needs.*

I've kept that silver bell to remind me that he knows my wishes, too.

Ten Things You Can Say to Make Someone's Day

CATHERINE E. ROLLINS

The role of encourager is vital in our world today—and especially at Christmas, when weather can be dreary, when stress increases, when people without family ties can feel lonely. With so many people struggling with job loss, relationship loss, and loss of self-esteem, now more than ever may be the time when you can be the one who helps another person face her present and future with boldness and confidence.

We can bolster a friend's spirits by what we do—or by what we say. When you want to give someone a word of encouragement and don't know what to say, here are ten phrases to help bring new perspective to a discouraged friend's life.

1. "You Are Growing"

The discouraged person rarely has a sense of her own progress—as a person, in a relationship, or in a career. As her friend, you can see her growth and call attention to it. Be specific. Point out trends you see over weeks or months.

Behavior that has changed. Say, "Last year you would have blown up in anger at that statement. You really handled it well today."

Physical attributes that have changed.

"Three months ago you weighed fifteen pounds more than you do now!"

New habits that have been established. "Six months ago you weren't praying at all. Now you're setting aside time every day for devotions."

New skills that have been acquired. "You had never even turned on a computer two months ago. Look at you now!"

2. "You May Be Down, but You're Not Out"

Many circumstances in life truly are "the pits." Your discouraged friend, however, tends to view her future like the present. You can help her see that one day she *will* be able to function better than she can at present.

Discuss with your friend her definition of well-being. For example, ask:

"What are you hoping to be able to do next month that you can't do now?"

"How would you like to be living at this time next year?"

Encourage your friend to write down a few goals for future reference. Focusing on a brighter tomorrow helps a person get past a gloomy today!

3. "You Have Options"

The discouraged person often feels as if she's reached the end of the road. Help your friend see that there's at least one way out of her situation—and probably more. With your friend's help, identify as many options as possible. Don't dismiss anything as being too absurd. In fact, go for the far-fetched! It will help you both laugh. Off-the-wall ideas frequently trigger truly creative options.

Once you've listed a wide variety of options, evaluate each one for its feasibility, material or physical cost, and outcome. Next, rank the options and decide on "Plan A." Help your friend figure out how to implement her chosen option. Consider timing, methods, and other prerequisites that need to be in place for success—including people, resources, and information.

4. "You Did Really Well"

Find something you can applaud genuinely and be generous in doing so:

"That was great!"

"I really enjoyed your performance."

"You had me in stitches."

"I was delighted to hear your ideas!"

Don't overlook "small" performances. Let a coworker know you appreciate a well-made presentation or an accurately typed letter. Let a roommate know you appreciate the way she completed a chore or prepared a special meal. Compliment your friend's appearance, choices, suggestions, or efforts.

5. "I Forgive You"

Guilt weighs heavy on the soul. Three of the most encouraging words you can offer a friend are, "I forgive you."

Forgiveness frees. It restores. It heals. If your friend is bemoaning her failures, mistakes, or sins, say, "I don't hold this against you," or "Ask forgiveness of the one you've wronged, then forgive yourself. Move forward in your life and leave this behind you."

6. "One Thing I Really Admire about You Is . . ."

Most of us are taught from an early age not to think more highly of ourselves than we ought. However, it's quite acceptable to recognize our good points and value them. Your friend probably has lost sight of some of her fine qualities. Point out her strengths, including:

Natural talents and interests. What comes easily for her? What does she have a natural interest in doing? Draw on past experience and listen for statements from your friend such as "I always wanted to . . ." or "I wish I had . . ."

Personal traits. What about her is attractive to others? Be sure to go beyond appearance. Cite those personality traits that you find compelling.

7. "Here Is Something That Spoke to Me of You"

Pass along uplifting words you encounter, overhear, or read. They may be a passage of poetry, a verse of Scripture, the message on a bumper sticker, a lighthearted story in a newspaper, a slogan on a coffee mug seen at a roadside cafe. Let your friend know you were thinking of her in a positive way.

If the words are something you can cut out, do so. Write in the margin, "I hope this brings a smile. I thought of you when I read this."

Be especially attuned to articles that relate to her interests, work, or projects.

8. "It's Never Too Late to Make a Change"

A fast-forward person can have a sense of loss or discouragement about her inability to afford life's necessities with less effort or a less-hurried pace.

As a result, she feels she has no control over her daily regimen. To a discouraged friend who is stressed

or burned out by the hectic pace she keeps, your encouraging word may well be, "It's never too late to make a change."

9. "You're Not Alone"

Help your friend realize she's not the only person to have encountered a specific circumstance or problem. Encourage her to find a support group of people who have faced the fact that they are having difficulty solving a problem on their own. Your friend will feel less isolated and will gain constructive information to help her work through her problem. In addition to support groups, stories of fellow strugglers also are available in books, movies, and videotapes.

Even if your friend has a unique problem, you can encourage her that she is not alone—you are choosing to be in the midst of the problem with her! You may not be able to advise your friend from your own experience or training, but you can assure her that you are there to "walk through the emotions" with her.

10. "You Are One of a Kind"

No other person can duplicate your friend's birth, childhood, and circumstances—not even a twin! Nobody has your friend's unique opportunities in life or processes information in exactly the way she does. Nobody has her combination of talents, insights, or skills.

Point out the ways your friend is truly "one of a kind." Highlight the fact she has a unique set of friends and a unique purpose in life in God's plan. Encourage your friend by saying, "There has never been and there never will be another person just like you—and I'm glad about that. I count it a great privilege to know you in all your uniqueness!"

No matter how sincere you are, some people do *not* receive encouragement. Keep in mind that your friend must be open to the idea of encouragement in order for you to encourage her. Don't let your failure to encourage a friend result in your own discouragement! Another friend needs your words of encouragement, even if she appears to be on top of the world. The truth is, *everybody* needs encouragement!

The encouragement you give tends to come back to you in like measure. Encouragement can become a cycle that generates joy, promotes wholeness, and gives strength—to others as well as to yourself.

HOLIDAY HAND-ME-DOWNS

The Sunday before Christmas, my Sunday school class brought me gifts. One little girl presented her package and innocently said, "Here, someone gave this to my mommy, and she didn't want it."

ALISON DENIGHT

Gift Horse

DEBBIE MEECE, as told to Holly G. Miller

Four years ago in December, I spent weeks talking about a beautiful horse I had discovered while searching for a stablemate for my aging childhood horse, Truly Fair. I had often dreamed of the day when our children, Kelly and Christopher, might share my lifelong interest in horses and learn the discipline and responsibility that come from caring for them. But the dream faded one night over dinner when my husband, David, confirmed what I already knew: We couldn't afford another horse. I promised myself never again to speak of the horse.

In the days leading up to that Christmas, I focused on the true meaning of the season. I thought about how God had chosen to send out his Son not in the majestic garb of a king but in the swaddling clothes of a common man. I remembered hearing that evidence of God's grace is everywhere—even in a stable. *What a place to find God's grace!* I thought.

The concept of grace had always been hard for me to grasp. I could recite its definition, "an unmerited gift from God," but knowing it in my head and understanding it in my heart were two different things. Surely I wasn't worthy of receiving such an "unmerited" gift as God's Son. That was beyond my comprehension.

On Christmas morning, after we had exchanged our presents, David and the children approached me with a final package that hadn't been under the tree. Their eyes glowed with anticipation as they watched me slowly loosen the red ribbon. There inside was a box inside a box. At the bottom, hidden in tissue paper, was a snapshot. I did a double take as I recognized the graceful horse I had befriended weeks earlier. I felt overwhelmed that David would give me a horse when we couldn't afford one.

That night, when I was in the stable feeding Truly Fair, I thought of Jesus and how he was born in a stable with only a bed of prickly hay. "Evidence of God's grace really *is* everywhere," I whispered, remembering the anticipation in David's eyes as he presented me with his gift. I wondered if that is how God feels. Does he wait expectantly for each of us to accept his gift of Jesus and of eternal life? Does he think, *I've already chosen your gift, and I can't wait to give him to you?*

The scent of hay and grain sweetened the air in the stable as I thought of my gift horse. My heart confirmed what my head was thinking: *What a place to find God's grace!*

Gifts of the Spirit

MARSHA CROCKETT

Not all Christmas gifts come wrapped in ribbon. Take a lesson in gift giving from Bible characters who gave the greatest gifts of all. Then use your imagination to make them a reality for your holiday season.

The Gift of Blessing

The prophet Simeon offered blessings to the baby Jesus and his parents (Luke 2:25-35). Your blessings too can greatly influence the lives of others when shared in these fun-to-give ways:

1. Write a love letter to your spouse.

2. Frame your child's name and its meaning.

3. Give a memory back to your parents by recording or writing about a shared event that was most meaningful in your life.

The Gift of Support

Like Aaron and Hur upholding the hands of Moses (Exod. 17:10-13), offer your friendship and support to someone who may be left alone this Christmas:

1. Take a picnic lunch to share with a shut-in or nursing-home resident.

2. Send a letter to an out-of-town friend struggling with a difficult problem.

3. Invite a single parent and child to join your family during the holidays.

The Gift of Sacrifice

Christ pointed to a widow giving her last coin as an example of superior giving (Luke 21:3-4). Our sacrifices can offer new meaning to the word *gift*:

1. Offer a day or night of free baby-sitting to a homemaker and her husband.

2. Give up your weekly workout time and surprise the kids with a trip to the park.

3. Give your silk scarf or gold necklace to the daughter, sister, or good friend who always asks to borrow it.

The Gift of Symbolism

Give symbolic gifts, like those the Wise Men gave (Matt. 2:11), to your loved ones this Christmas:

1. A ring to symbolize a circle of friendship.

2. A beribboned candle to tell someone how she brings light and happiness into your life.

3. A start from a houseplant to represent a life rooted in Christ's love.

4. Seeds for an herb garden to symbolize hope or a new and changed life with Christ.

Traditions WITH A TWIST

Five years ago, after experiencing several stressful Christmases in a row because of last-minute shopping, I decided to make a change. Now I shop for Christmas gifts all year-round. Preplanning my gift giving helps me focus on each person on my list so that I purchase or make a *uniquely suited* gift, instead of rushing just to get *any* gift. It also takes away the anxiety of having to find gifts in crowded malls after Thanksgiving. For the past five holidays, I've been able to focus on the *real* event and meaning behind Christmas—Jesus Christ, who came to earth to die for our sins, so that we might live eternally.

FAITH CRAMER

My Favorite Christmas Gift

*What is your most memorable Christmas present? Perhaps it is the sacrifice of a
parent during lean years, the sentiment of a spouse reaffirming his love, the faithfulness
of a longtime friend sending that perfect present across the miles.
As you read the following stories from others' treasure chests, reflect on your own
cherished memories. Maybe this Christmas is even a good time for you to jot them
down to inspire the next generation!*

Decades of Friendship

I have a very close friend whom I've known since 1969, when we were both seven
years old. When we were thirteen, we had a big argument just before Christmas. I
felt bad about the disagreement, so I bought her a small book titled *Christmas Is a Time
for Friends*—with lovely photos and prose about the beauty of friendship at Christmas.
Inside the front cover I wrote "Merry Christmas in '75" and signed my name.

We settled our differences and continued our friendship, despite the fact that our lives
took very different paths: I went off to college, then got a job away from our
hometown; she married and began raising her family. Yet we've stayed best friends and
always manage to get together at Christmas. In 1985, I received a touching gift from
her—the very same book I'd given her ten years earlier! Inside the front cover, under
my original inscription, she'd written "Merry Christmas in '85" and signed her name.

This little book has become a symbol of the enduring friendship we've enjoyed. In
1995, I had the privilege of wrapping up that same book and giving it back to my
best friend with the simple inscription "Merry Christmas in '95"! *TERRI L. THOMAS*

Handmade Treasures

I was ten years old the Christmas after my dad chose to divorce my mom and
move 150 miles away. In order to make ends meet, we moved into a
century-old house, and Mom was forced to go to work checking groceries at a
nearby market. I can only imagine how Mom's heart must have ached as she
watched my two sisters, my brother, and me pore over our wish lists for Dad,
all the while knowing the financial destitution she faced that holiday season.

62

Yet under the tree that Christmas morning were four personalized footstools made of logs—taken from our woodpile where Mom spent her lunch hour every day chopping wood for the stove. They were peeled and painted with leftover house paint, and our names were printed on the front with nail polish.

The toys that Dad bought us eventually broke and were cast aside, but the stools remained sturdy and lasted a long time. That year, I learned Christmas isn't found in packages under a tree but in the hearts of people—in a mother's love for her children, in the giving of oneself for another. *JUDY MILLER*

Renewed Vows

My husband, Mike, and I have been married nineteen years. It's a second marriage for both of us, and we each brought two children into our family. As the years passed, the children grew up and left home for college, marriage, and the navy. In 1992, I told our children how much I wanted all of them home for Christmas the next year.

The much anticipated time finally arrived, and we had fun sharing Christmas memories. As we finished exchanging gifts, Mike told everyone we had one more gift for them and that they needed to be ready for it at 11:00 A.M. He'd rented a limousine to pick us up for a drive downtown, at which time we planned to give them each their last gift—a card with money in it.

As we were riding in the limo, Mike surprised me by handing me a lovely card. After I'd read it, he asked me if I would marry him again. With tears streaming down my cheeks, I said yes. Then the limo pulled up in front of the Little White Chapel, and he told me that we were going to renew our vows.

Mike had made all the arrangements. My son escorted me down the aisle and gave me away, and then all four children and their mates stood with us as we restated our vows—my most special Christmas gift ever. *JUDY D. HALLGREN*

Letter Legacy

I met my friend Mary five years ago through a support-group newsletter when we were both struggling with infertility. Our names were matched as prayer partners, and through our correspondence we became friends. We live only 130 miles apart, so occasional visits are easy to arrange, but we've written each other many letters over the years. Although we've exchanged

Christmas gifts since our first year of friendship, the gift she gave me this past year was quite special. The box contained photocopies of every letter I'd written to her, arranged in chronological order! Now I have a treasured journal of my life for the years I've known her. *DIANA COLLIER*

Belated Barbie
My dad was a pastor and the father of five, so money was tight when I was young. We had plenty on the table, and birthdays and Christmas were always fun, but somehow, my twin sister and I never received a Barbie doll.

One day I was talking with my adult friends about missing out on this doll, and Mike, my nine-year-old son, heard the longing in my voice.

On Christmas morning, he was bursting with anticipation for me to open my gifts. When I opened his package and found a Tropical Barbie, I first thought he'd mixed up the labels and that it must be meant for his four-year-old sister, Jillian. But one look at his face told me this was his special gift for *me*. He kissed me and said, "This is so you won't be sad anymore for never having a Barbie." I cried and thanked him profusely. No gift has ever meant more to me. I'll always remember this special present, given straight from my son's heart. *SHERRI WARD*

Grandma's Bequest
Christmas Day 1982 was difficult for my family and me because my grandmother had passed away just three weeks before. As the gifts were handed out, I was given a small box labeled "To Kris, Love Grammy." I looked at my parents, thinking they'd purchased it to lift my heavy heart. They assured me this gift was indeed from my grandmother.

I opened the gift with tears in my eyes and found a beautiful, dainty, silver crucifix necklace. It was as if my grandmother were continuing to share her love of the Lord with me, even beyond heaven's gates! *KRISTEN MARUSICH*

Band of Gold
My husband, Bobby, and I have been married sixteen years and have had our share of struggles. We rededicated our lives to Christ a few years ago. Our renewed commitment to the Lord and each other strengthened our marriage considerably.

Bobby had lost his wedding band back in the early eighties and really didn't have a desire to wear jewelry anyway. Last year, in my Christmas stocking, I found a little box that contained a wedding band—for Bobby, from Bobby. With it was a letter he'd written, apologizing for all the years he'd not worn a ring and saying he wanted to wear one now to show how happy he was that God had chosen us to share our lives together. As I slipped the ring on his finger, I'm sure I was the happiest woman in the world. *KATHY JACKSON*

The Gift of Life

My husband and I had longed for a baby for more than ten years, and every Christmas we thought about how wonderful it would be to see this special holiday through a child's eyes.

Then in 1988, a woman named Bobbie was unable to keep the baby she was to deliver in September, and God arranged for my husband and me to be chosen as the parents of her child.

On Christmas Day, we dedicated our three-month-old son, Kyle, to the Lord. What a blessed gift a total stranger gave us that Christmas—the unselfish act of giving up her firstborn child. She'll never know how much her gift has meant to my husband and me, but I know God will bless her richly for it. *BONNIE STANDARD*

Home Cooking

As my husband and I sought to establish a weekly newspaper in Michigan, we struggled to keep our heads above water. We put everything we had into the effort, and as a result we lived in an apartment with no kitchen. We cooked on a camp stove and used the cold Michigan temperatures outside our window as an icebox. I'd set a goal of buying a microwave oven to help with meal preparations, but then a bill had to be paid, and the fund for my microwave disappeared. We didn't even have the money to go home for Christmas until a check, specifically designated as gas money, arrived from my grandmother.

Our visit was a warm source of encouragement. After Christmas dinner, we all gathered in the living room to open gifts. When there was only one large box left, Mom slid it over to me and grinned. Inside was the microwave I'd been trying to buy for myself.

Almost ten years have passed since then—and the newspaper effort didn't succeed. God called us into ministry and blessed us with two girls my mom didn't live to see. But the microwave still sits on my kitchen counter, and Mom still helps me get dinner a couple times a week. *BARBARA BEADERSTADT*

Surprise Santa

My sister, Dana, and I received plaster Santa banks about forty years ago when we were young children. Unfortunately, most of my belongings—especially my favorite Christmas decorations—were destroyed by fire resulting from an earthquake in 1989.

That Christmas, I opened a box from my sister and was amazed to see the plump, cheery face of my Santa bank. I thought that somehow she'd been able to find the replacement I'd been unsuccessfully hunting for at antique shops and flea markets. Imagine my added delight when she said it was *her* bank. She wanted me to have it since I'd lost so much in the fire.

That worn, plaster bank renewed my hope and deepened my love for my sister and for our precious Lord Jesus—whose love shone through her giving this present. *MARCENE Y. SAXMAN*

Life-Sized Love

My father died when I was four, forcing my young mother to get a job as a school cook. The blessing of getting off work before we arrived home was more than a fair trade for a meager income.

When I was seven, I asked for a life-sized doll with gorgeous, long blonde hair for Christmas. She was my height, and she walked when you took her hand. Mom tried to explain that, beautiful as "Mandy" was, she was way beyond our financial reach. After a few weeks of begging, pleading, and being as angelic as was childishly possible, I gave up.

At the crack of dawn that Christmas, my brother and I tore down the stairs. As I rounded the corner, I saw her—Mandy! She was too big to wrap, so Mom had put a lovely bow in the doll's hair and had propped her by the tree. Instead of rushing over and grabbing her, I just froze. I finally turned to see Mom standing in the doorway, a smile brighter than the Christmas lights across her face. I burst into tears—even at seven, I realized she had sacrificed for me. I've always loved my mother, but never more than at that moment. *ROXANNE HUSEMAN*

Back to the Bible

One December night at supper with my husband and teenage son, I mentioned I'd like an *Amplified Bible*, thinking my husband might take the hint. At the time, our son wasn't walking with the Lord and was avoiding "spiritual things."

However, when Christmas came and I opened my son's gift, I was surprised and overjoyed to find a lovely *Amplified Bible*, which he had bought with his own money and signed with a touching inscription. That beloved Bible continues to be a special treasure. Today, my son's been living for the Lord more than ten years—and is now teaching his sons about the Bible. *PHYLLIS TUCKER*

Door to Door

Marie and her family moved in next door two months after my family and I moved in. Our kids are the same ages, and Marie and I quickly grew to be good friends. We've laughed and cried together, gotten angry and forgiven each other, and even joked about building an addition to connect our houses.

One year, she invited our family over for Christmas. Our children had always exchanged gifts, so I expected the tradition to continue. But I was surprised when, after the children had opened their presents, she handed me a large box. Inside was a beautiful wooden plaque for our front door with my family's name and a cross carved in it.

Although Marie had never been very open about her faith, that day I saw tears in her eyes. Her gift was evidence that God had reached through me to touch her with his truth and love. Now all who knock on our door know the Wilcox family lives here—and so does Jesus. *BARBARA WILCOX*

A Gift Worth Repeating

MAYO MATHERS

"What's the best Christmas present you've ever received?" someone asked me recently. It took me only a few moments to respond. My favorite gift, though delivered by a neighbor, came straight from God at a time when I was grieving the loss of a family friend.

Ralph was a forty-four-year-old father of five. We had invested fifteen years into weaving our two families together into a sturdy fabric of friendship. While he and his family were moving into a new home, Ralph suddenly died of a heart attack, catapulting us into a state of profound shock.

Our family quickly gathered up Ralph's wife, Sandee, and their children and brought them to our home. Through the numbness we helped Sandee face the endless details surrounding her husband's death.

Meanwhile, our house bulged with people as their friends and out-of-town relatives arrived for the funeral. We set up camping trailers in our driveway and rolled out sleeping bags in the house. Caring for everyone was a welcome distraction, yet my increasing weariness made it more and more difficult.

The morning of the funeral, I woke up to find Ralph's elderly father standing over me. "Eh! Eh!" he said, pointing toward the kitchen. A recent stroke had robbed him of the ability to communicate, but I understood he wanted breakfast.

Every muscle in my body screamed as I struggled to my feet. Even the simple task of perking coffee seemed a gigantic chore. *How can I possibly manage to feed the nearly thirty people asleep under my roof?* I groaned inwardly. A balloon of panic inflated inside me, threatening to burst.

Oh, God . . . I was too weary even to finish the prayer as I looked around my kitchen. Every inch of counter space was stacked with the cakes, pies, and bags of chips friends had been bringing for four days. My refrigerator brimmed with casseroles and salads. I could feed the whole town with this food—but none of it was suitable for breakfast.

The phone rang, and I lunged for the distraction it offered.

"What's for breakfast?" chirped the cheerful voice on the other end.

Another person to feed! I thought in despair. As I stammered, the voice I now recognized to be my next-door neighbor's interrupted. "Don't fix a thing. I just took two pans of homemade cinnamon rolls out of the oven. I thought you might need them."

A few minutes later, my house was filled with the savory odor of cinnamon rolls—enough for everyone. I scooped one out and bit into its buttery warmth. *God saw my floundering and met my need!*

Since that morning, the spicy aroma of cinnamon rolls always reminds me of God's timely gift. For that reason, this Christmas I want to fill someone else's house with the spicy aroma of God's love. It's a gift worth repeating.

"I better not catch you kids shaking those gifts to try to figure out what they are."

The Most Thoughtful Gift I Ever Received

Inexpensive Gift Ideas

_____

_____

_____

_____

_____

_____

_____

_____

_____

_____

_____

_____

_____

_____

_____

_____

_____

_____

_____

_____

_____

_____

_____

_____

_____

_____

_____

Notes about Nifty Gift-Wraps

True Hospitality: Making Others Feel Kindly Welcome

Christmas has arrived—the time of year when, most likely, you have more scheduled activities and "to do" lists than you do the entire rest of the year! How, at this busy season, can you still be a loving and unfrazzled host or hostess? It all comes from remembering this golden rule: Hospitality is not entertainment; hospitality is making people feel "kindly welcome," as the Shaker motto puts it. As we keep that in mind, we can focus on enjoying our guests rather than cooking elaborate food or decorating our home so it could appear in *Better Homes and Gardens*.

There is a myriad of options available about what we can do with our lives and the gifts God's given us, but there are not many role models who can show us how to juggle all these opportunities. Finding a healthy balance between all these possibilities is our biggest challenge.

ELISA MORGAN

Rachael Crabb: Hospitality on the Run

JANE JOHNSON STRUCK

"Today we're more concerned about locking our doors than bringing people into our homes," says Rachael Crabb, author of *The Personal Touch*, a practical book on biblical hospitality, and wife of Christian psychologist Larry Crabb. "Yet even in the end times, when the 'love of most will grow cold,' we still need to be hospitable to believers and non-Christians alike." The insights in her book reflect the wealth of experience Rachael has had in practicing the ministry of hospitality.

"When I grew up, we always had missionaries staying with us," explains Rachael. "And Larry and I have had a very open home. When our children were young, we'd have weekly neighborhood potlucks where we'd alternate homes. And our boys enjoyed being around all the different people. What a mind-stretcher it is to sit around your table and hear others share how God is working in their lives!"

Rachael readily admits that despite her love of hospitality, she does hate housework. "People who read my book send me easy recipes because they know how I hate to cook," she says with a laugh. "Fortunately, there aren't any rules that apply. Hospitality isn't about linen tablecloths; it's about giving—giving of yourself to others. I like to say, 'People are more important—so let's have a good time!'"

Rachael is quick to emphasize that "other-centeredness"—not organizational skills or a *House Beautiful* home—is the necessary ingredient for effective outreach.

"It's easy to be overwhelmed at the prospect of offering hospitality," Rachael says. "We all feel overscheduled at times. But even the most harried woman can give of herself in small but effective ways. The key is to care, to let others see a bit of Christ shining through."

Some nonthreatening methods of practicing hospitality don't even need to take place in the home, suggests Rachael. "You're never too busy to drop a postcard to someone who needs encouraging," she says. To help ease entertaining jitters, Rachael recommends teaming up with someone more experienced to host that first get-together.

"Christian women just don't have a choice about whether or not they'll be hospitable," says Rachael. "It's a biblical command. Scripture tells us that in the last days, people will be lovers of themselves. We're called to be givers instead."

Traditions WITH A TWIST

I'm thirty-five and single—and for many years the Advent wreath, candles, and special decorations I had from childhood lay in the bottom of my hope chest, waiting for "someday."

About five years ago, I decided I was done waiting. So my sister—who's also my roommate—and I started a new tradition. We each have a number of single friends who are very active in their respective churches. Advent tends to be a hectic time, so we don't see much of each other.

Now everyone knows that on the four Sunday evenings preceding Christmas, we host an open house. Our friends drop by after church, choir practice, or shopping, and enjoy carols, candlelight, and hot chocolate or cider. After several have arrived, we have a brief devotion, light the appropriate Advent candle, and pray together. It's a quiet way to end a frantic week and prepares us for the week ahead.

I'd still love to have a true family Christmas, but in the meantime, these friends are "family," and my sister and I look forward to continuing our own special Christmas tradition every year.

GINGER WEAVER

"Maybe we should turn the heat up . . ."

Old-Fashioned Advice for Today

DENISE TURNER

My grandmother was the most hospitable person I have ever known. People dropped by her house every day for a piece of her home-baked coconut cake. When people drop by my house, I'm usually not home—and I don't even know how to bake coconut cake. That used to bother me until the day I caught my grandmother sneaking a cake mix into her kitchen cupboard. "These things are every bit as moist as mine," she said with a giggle. "The only reason I didn't use them fifty years ago is because nobody had thought them up."

Why was Grandmother such a wonderful hostess? The reasons probably have little to do with the meals she prepared. Here's some of the sage wisdom about hospitality I've gleaned from the grandmothers I've known.

Grandmother was not the world's most perfect homemaker. She wasn't a trained gourmet cook either. So you might as well forget about getting elaborate recipes from her. Instead, concentrate on her favorite tips like, "Cook with the freshest fruits and vegetables you can get," or "Simple, basic foods are best."

Grandmother was genuinely happy to see everyone—and thus everyone seemed to congregate on her doorstep. The perennial "open house" may be out of style today. Yet we can still dedicate our homes to God and carry on Grandmother's attitude of love for people.

Grandmother's gift of hospitality did not depend on large amounts of money. This was evidenced by the fact that she always insisted she liked the chicken backs best. Of course, the wealthier you are, the more elegant your entertaining style can be. But how many of your friends genuinely prefer caviar to vegetables and dip?

Grandmother did make the best gingerbread cookies in the world. However, most people remember the gingery smell of Grandmother's house more clearly than the exact taste of the cookies. It was an atmosphere she created that people remember with fondness.

Of course, it's impossible to recreate the "good old days," and we probably wouldn't be happy living Grandmother's life, even if we could. But we can combine the best of the old with the best of the new.

Grandmother's special brand of hospitality is summed up in an old Shaker motto, "We make you kindly welcome." The Shakers follow these simple rules of hospitality: Keep hot food hot and cold food cold—and always give your hands to work and your heart to God.

Some ideas never go out of style.

The Christmas I Spent with Strangers

RAMONA CRAMER TUCKER

There's "no place like home"—especially during the holidays. But I'll never forget the Christmas I spent with total strangers.

I was a college senior, en route with my sister and her husband to our parents' home in Canada when a fierce snowstorm struck. Within minutes our compact car, laden with packages, slid into a ditch.

After fruitless shoveling, we huddled together under blankets in the backseat—and prayed. We knew our chances of being rescued quickly in such dangerous weather were slim.

But a few hours later, we heard a knock on our car roof. Our rescuer, who "just happened" to be the only tow-truck driver in town, ended up taking us to his parents' home to spend the night.

On Christmas morning, we awoke to find stockings filled with goodies—for us! Afterward, our rescuer towed the car to his shop and checked it over. That afternoon, as we drove off, the family accepted our grateful thank-you's with, "We were stranded a few years back, and someone helped us."

We finally arrived in Canada two days later—and the joy we felt at being home surpassed any holiday we'd ever shared.

That was twelve years ago. Since then, the first Christmas card I send every year goes to that family, who took in three strangers during the busiest season of all!

Entertaining with Style

JANE JOHNSON STRUCK

You don't need damask, Waterford, and Wedgwood to entertain with style. Here are some ideas for simply elegant entertaining:

1. *Bring out your best for your friends.* Don't save your best crystal, china, and silver (if you have them) only for holidays or that rare "the boss is coming for dinner" dinner. Everyday dishes can be just as festive if you use colorful place mats, a striking centerpiece, or creative napkin folding. And don't forget the candles!

2. *Build your party around a specific theme.* Some themes are obvious—Valentine's Day, a birthday. Or take your cue from the season or the menu. Then decorate accordingly. At your local library, you'll find entertaining guides filled with useful and inexpensive ideas for delightful decorating schemes. "I like to add something of interest to each party I give," my friend Dede says. It may be a personalized Christmas ornament at each place setting or some other unique touch to make the evening memorable.

3. *Use place cards to prevent that "sit anywhere" confusion.* Designate seating arrangements with small cards—white for formal occasions, colored for casual. Or tie them in with your party theme.

4. *Avoid seating married couples together.* This is their chance to get acquainted with others. They can sit together at home!

5. *Set your table properly.* Flatware is arranged according to its order of usage with the first piece on the outside, working in (forks left of plate, knives then spoons to right). Napkins are placed either to the left or on the dinner plate. Goblets, glasses, and coffee cups sit above the knives.

6. *Stay flexible.* You may not have enough "bread and butter" plates to serve eight or twelve matching dinner plates. Mix and match with an eye to color and pattern, and you'll set a pretty and interesting table.

Making Guests Feel at Ease

KATHY BENCE

Silence. The roomful of people you've invited over have nothing to say to each other. You panic, racking your brain for a way to break the ice.

Nearly every hostess has encountered those moments when it seems her guests, especially quiet ones, would rather be anywhere else but in her home. But a few uneasy moments need not drive you into a panic if you follow these tips:

How you regard others can make a difference. When talking to people, concentrate less on what they may think of you and more on getting to know them. There are so many things to discover about people—their dreams and goals, needs, sorrows, spiritual life, family relationships, job experiences, hobbies, cultural preferences, even their family origins.

Call people by name as you talk. Using people's names helps them feel accepted.

Give guests small jobs to do, if they ask. Helping you prepare a salad or set the table may allow them time to overcome their shyness and nervousness.

Create a comfortable setting in your house. Build a fire in the fireplace. Put soothing music on the stereo. Use green plants to "soften" your living room. Evaluate your home: Is it too formal to be comfortable? Less-formal surroundings may help visitors relax.

Offer easy-to-eat hors d'oeuvres so your guests have something to do while getting acquainted.

Let your children become a part of your gathering. They usually befriend strangers more naturally than adults. And most guests will be delighted by their presence.

Ask someone gifted in drawing others out to talk to the most uncomfortable guest at your gathering.

If you don't know your guests, plan some simple activities. A drive in the country, a walk through your neighborhood, or working on a project everyone enjoys will help overcome any awkwardness.

Keep these questions in mind for times when the conversation lags:

How do you like living in this area?

Where did you grow up?

Tell me about your job.

For you, what was the highlight of this past year? the Christmas season? your life?

Who has had the greatest influence on your spiritual life?

What activity interests you the most and why?

If you could go overseas, which country would you like to visit? Why?

What is the best book you've been reading lately?

If money were no object, what would you be doing right now?

Remember, most people want to be known, but they may not know how to open up. Set an example by sharing freely from your own life. Then listen carefully as your quiet friends begin to follow your lead.

Traditions WITH A TWIST

Throughout the years, as friends and family have married and had children, the holidays have become increasingly hectic. After battling to find dates for an informal Christmas party, my husband and I chose instead to host a "white elephant" party on New Year's Eve, when schedules have slowed down. Our friends and family arrive around seven o'clock, and everyone brings a "munchie." We supply hot cider, punch, and several salty and sweet snacks. Each guest brings a "white elephant" gift, wrapped and ready to put under the tree. These gifts cannot be purchased; they must be found somewhere in your house or apartment. The goal is to come up with the most tacky, ridiculous gift you can find. Prizewinning gifts from past parties have been an ugly plaster chicken, a plastic fireman's hat, a stair bannister from a remodeling project, and a headband with Christmas lights attached. Upon arrival, each person receives a number and chooses a gift under the tree in order of the number he or she receives. There is much hysterical laughter, and some of the "treasures" are even "stolen" by those who really want them. Next, we read a Christmas story and watch a funny Christmas movie. Shortly before midnight, we all share something we're thankful for in the past and something we're looking forward to in the future.

RAMONA CRAMER TUCKER

Getting Your Husband to Help

JANE JOHNSON STRUCK

It's 6:22 P.M. and you're frantically microwaving the kids' hot dogs as you pick up 181 Fisher-Price people from the family room you cleaned two hours ago. Company's due at 7:30 P.M.—and you haven't even showered yet! Worse—*somebody* forgot to make more ice cubes. Meanwhile, your husband blissfully shaves. You stifle a scream.

Sound familiar? Entertaining shouldn't require a showdown between the sexes. As *Creative Hospitality* author Marlene LeFever writes, "Hospitality is not a feminine work." So how can wives get their husbands more involved? Here are some suggestions:

Consider your husband's basic temperament. If he likes having large crowds over, great. But if he prefers small groups, stick with situations in which he's comfortable. My friend Dick admits it's hard to get keyed up for dressy dining. "I dress for success five days a week," he says. "On weekends I want to relax." If your husband faces work pressure or is feeling down, time out from socializing may be what he needs most. When the timing is right, your husband will be more apt to be a willing partner, not a reluctant participant.

Make your husband part of the plan. "Giving a party is something you both do," writes LeFever. "Jack and I plan together on ideas and in the end enjoy the party together."

Break your party up into three manageable stages: preparation, party, and postparty cleanup. Decide together what he's willing to tackle. My husband's more than willing to perform the manly rite of grilling burgers. Maybe your husband dices up a super salad. But if culinary arts aren't your husband's forte, perhaps "supervising" is. "My husband appointed himself V.P. of munchies," one wife says. "He makes sure our supply of peanuts or chips for our guests is replenished, because he likes to snack!"

Take the direct approach to asking for help. Marilyn's husband systematically cleans the bathroom before company arrives. "Ever since Dave remodeled our bathroom, he enjoys cleaning it," she explains. But alas, your husband may not demonstrate an affinity for toilet bowl cleaning. Maybe he's more like Michael, who, according to his wife, "shines when it comes to mealtime conversation but never thinks to ask, 'Need some help?' while I'm struggling with the vacuum." Politely request assistance with specific tasks and give a deadline: "Could you please vacuum the living room before six o'clock?"

Strategically placed checklists (taped to the fridge or TV) communicate without nagging. Ask your husband to sign up for items he feels interested in.

Keep in mind that husbands are your partners in the ministry of hospitality, not mind readers. Be honest about your concerns and your expectations for the evening, but be patient too. With careful planning, open communication, and willing ears, you'll both share the work—and the rewards—of entertaining.

"Now if you're still cold, I'll throw another blanket on the bed."

Mother's Little Helpers

KATHY BENCE

When entertaining becomes a family affair, children discover the joy of serving others—and they feel good about themselves, too.

Why not get your children involved in your next holiday get-together? Be sure to allow extra time to supervise them during the event. And assign them tasks according to age and ability.

Children under Ten Can:

- pick flowers for the table
- choose and arrange seating
- draw creative place cards for guests
- set the table
- butter the bread
- give their opinions about the menu
- serve appetizers (if they aren't spillable)
- crack and beat eggs
- create centerpieces (with supervision)
- greet guests at the door
- knead dough in a child-sized pan

Children over Ten Can:

- help elderly guests to the table
- cook with simple recipes
- assemble easy-to-prepare hors d'oeuvres
- act as a host/hostess or waiter/waitress
- hang up coats
- clear the dishes after the meal
- do anything on the list for "Children under Ten"

By allowing your children to help, you are really developing their sense of self-worth and responsibility. And you are giving them cherished memories they can one day build on as they create their own family traditions.

We are the hands and feet of Christ. We need to do what Christ would do. If people are hungry, feed them. If they're lonely, talk to them. If they're discouraged, encourage them. Do it by whatever means you can—if you can bake, take them some banana bread. If you can read, then go to the youth detention center and read to the people there. Do what you can to make a difference in somebody's life—one life at a time, right here at home.

BABBIE MASON

Win the Prize for "Best Guest"

JANE JOHNSON STRUCK

Your bags are packed, and you're on your way to a weeklong stay with your in-laws over the holidays. Or you're preparing to visit old college friends for a much-anticipated weekend. What attitudes and insights can you take with you to guarantee that your time as a guest leaves behind special memories? Here are tips to help you master the art of being a hospitable guest.

Respect your hosts' privacy. Even the most congenial of relationships requires breathing room amidst shared quarters. "When my mom visits," observes my friend Heather, "she spends chunks of time in her room reading or writing letters." The end result, admits Heather, is something both hosts and guests need throughout the duration of any visit—time alone.

Go with the family flow. Each family establishes its own schedule. A hospitable guest recognizes these patterns and fits in. Our family members, for example, like to shower in the morning. Visiting relatives thoughtfully shower in the evenings to avoid early morning bathroom bottlenecks. Devise your own strategy to avoid disrupting your hosts' usual routine.

Be specific with your offers of help. Says my friend Koby, "When someone asks me, 'Is there something I can do to help?' my natural response is, 'No thanks, just relax.' But if a guest asks, 'Can I make the salad?' or 'Can I strip the beds?' I say, 'Great!'" Guests who focus on specific tasks eliminate the hosts' need to devise "something for them to do."

Remember that in the kitchen, no help may be the best help of all. Be sensitive to your hosts' feelings. While some may love a crowded kitchen, for others "too many cooks spoil the broth." If so, assist by keeping children from getting underfoot during meal preparation. Or keep the conversational fires burning in the living room while cleanup is underway in the kitchen. Your hosts will appreciate your tact.

Don't forget to say thanks creatively. Thank-you gifts need not be fancy or expensive. My favorite present is a centerpiece of dried flowers crafted lovingly by a former college roommate who visited us briefly several years ago. It still sits on my table and reminds me of her. Sometimes the gift of time—an offer to baby-sit for the hosts—will be well received. "An African family that lived with us awhile thanked us by presenting us with a special painting," says Heather. "We see it hanging up and think of the times we shared." Whatever your idea, the gift should express genuine gratitude for your hosts' hospitality.

V I E W P O I N T S

How do you practice hospitality to neighbors, friends, or coworkers during the Christmas season? Here's what seven women said:

"I invite a friend over for lunch, often on the spur of the moment. If she's a career woman, it gives her a break from the office and the fast-food routine. If she's an at-home mom like me, it gives the kids a nice diversion and allows us a chance for some adult conversation. I keep the menu simple and the setting relaxed; it's the company that counts!" *KATHY AMES*

"I've met many friends at work, church, and school. Each month I invite two or three women who don't know each other to my home for coffee. Sometimes they each bring an ingredient, and we make a meal together. This way, friends from different parts of my life get to meet each other—and I'm not overwhelmed by entertaining." *MARIE LYN*

"Last Christmas, my husband and I invited ten people from our apartment building to come over for cookies and cider. We didn't expect a big showing, since these people really didn't know us except to say hello at the mailbox or in the parking lot. But all ten came! By the end of the evening, we were exchanging phone numbers. Since then, my husband and I have shared our faith with several of those neighbors. We've learned a little hospitality goes a long way. There are many *lonely* people in this world—many just next door." *ANNIE STEIN*

"When I see a new employee at work, I introduce myself and invite her to join me for lunch in our company cafeteria. To break the ice, I bring along a word game or magazine questionnaire and encourage everyone around the table to participate. New people find it easy to join in, and they get to meet coworkers from other departments." *CYNTHIA THOMAS*

"I used to think that because I'm in college, the practice of hospitality would have to wait until I had my own house. But I've learned God isn't bound by our circumstances. My roommate and I often keep our dorm room door open as an invitation for the girls on our hall to come in and talk. (Having chips and pop readily available doesn't hurt, either!) Privacy has become rare, but we've found that building relationships is worth it." *DEBRA J. WEINHEIMER*

"We often hear that singles feel left out socially at our church. So my husband and I make a special effort to entertain single men and women by inviting them over for dinner and a concert in the park or a trip to the museum. We consciously keep from talking about our kids and try to center the conversation on mutual interests. The relationships that have developed have been rich and rewarding." *NANCY JOHNSON*

"No one came to see us when we moved into our new neighborhood, so we decided to have an open house. Since we didn't know names, we placed invitations in each neighbor's mailbox. We drew a plan of our neighborhood on poster board, and as the neighbors arrived, we had them fill in their name, address, and phone number on the space for their house. Everyone enjoyed themselves and wondered why it took a new neighbor to bring them together." *RUTH ANN POTTS*

No Time to Entertain

LAURETTA PATTERSON

My friend's voice on the other end of the line was taut, strained. Words poured out in a rush. "I didn't know who to call. I'm scared! My neighbor's children have to be hidden from their father for their own safety. We've got to move quickly! Can I bring them over to your house right now?"

Somehow, it wasn't supposed to be like this. Lounging in the serenity of my hospital bed the night before, I had envisioned my son's homecoming filled with the joys only a newborn can bring. I had imagined our family lying on the big bed together examining Andy's fingers and toes or cuddling in front of a roaring fire.

Now this. Serve as a house of safety for a family in trouble? Not in my plan! Yet the moment was now; the need was immediate.

Sometimes, our call to be hospitable may come as a sudden surprise. Yet life in the 1990s fights against this sort of open-armed welcome. We are a generation of women flailing about in a morass of changing roles and expectations. Many of us struggle valiantly to juggle homes and careers, children's science projects, and the report due on the boss's desk. As we attempt to maintain an equilibrium in our own families, our focus narrows. "Cocooning," that notion of insulating ourselves for the sake of survival, seems to be the logical choice, given the clamoring demands on our time and lives.

And if we *should* venture into the world of entertaining, we're bombarded with expectations that stop us in our tracks! I recently walked into a local bookstore and found myself in what appeared to be the fairy-tale section. A collection of books on gracious entertaining lined the shelves. One book cover in particular caught my eye: There stood the hostess, elegantly dressed. Behind her sat a table laden with masterpieces for the eye and palate. The decorations? Her own. The fresh produce and herbs? From her garden, of course.

For many of us, such triumph is like something from the enchanted forest. We live instead in a world of plastic tablecloths, Ground Beef Delight, and wilted flower arrangements. Surely there's a lot to be said for gracious living—but as people of the 1990s, we are called to more than the pursuit of social niceties. Our hospitality should serve the lonely and broken of this world as well as build up believers to work for the kingdom.

Look at the hospitality shown by Publius, a chief official on the island where the apostle Paul landed, shipwrecked and snakebitten: "He [Publius] welcomed us to his home and for three days entertained us hospitably. . . . They honored us in many ways and when we were ready to sail, they furnished us with the supplies we needed" (Acts 28:7, 10). Publius couldn't help but notice the disheveled band of shipwrecked sailors and prisoners that showed up at his door. But the shipwrecked ones near us may not be so obvious. Surely the children of today's culture are among the adrift. Left to fend for themselves in a disintegrating world, they long for the safety of a friendly face or a place to belong.

I answered my doorbell one day to find a very earnest, wide-eyed little boy perched on my doorstep. With a quavery voice, he said, "My name's Billy, and I don't have *any* friends!" Soon my three boys had made him a regular member of their wooden-sword-fighting gang in our backyard.

But many of the lonely ones around us will not be so forthright in stating their needs. However, if our eyes are open, we'll notice them. Is there a single parent close by who needs a touch of relief and encouragement? How about an elderly neighbor who is fearful and lonely, or a disabled and isolated person desperate for contact with a friendly face?

It may not be only the lost and unbelieving who need a safe harbor. We're to "do good to all people, especially to . . . the family of believers" (Gal. 6:10), and to "show hospitality to such men [fellow Christians] so that we may work together for the truth" (3 John 8). Christians get worn out, too, and need an oasis where they can be loved, restored, fed, and prayed for.

We recently made a cross-country move that stretched us in ways both exhilarating and painful. After two years of relocation adjustments, we desperately needed a family vacation. Thank God for our own congregation's generosity and a British pastor and his family who understood our need and offered us the use of their cottage in England.

But when we arrived in England, we were a mess! Our bodies ached from jet lag and an unexpected London heat wave; tempers flared as our children's sticky elbows touched accidentally in the backseat of the tiny rental car. Heading west toward the Welsh border, we looked longingly for our destination and some sleep. Finally, when we pulled into our host's driveway, some gnawing doubts surfaced: "Suppose we overwhelm them? Suppose they find us to be obnoxious? What if we break things? This whole thing was a crazy idea!" Traveling with four children on a trip-of-a-lifetime had seemed like a better idea when we had been back home in America.

Then our host's door swung open. Beryl welcomed us with hugs. Seeing our flushed faces, she brought us out to the shady side of the house where we could enjoy the breeze, watch the sheep in the pasture, and delight in the ice cream and fresh fruit that appeared on a tray. An exhilarating moment—and a gracious beginning to the amazing hospitality our family received in the weeks to come.

Just as Publius welcomed Paul into his home, we can open wide the doors of our homes and declare, "Come on in! Be part of the family. Join the inner circle!" There is something profoundly intimate about being "let in" to another person's home. If you would ring my doorbell today and pop in for a cup of coffee, you would see a side of me that is different from the public side of me. You would see the scattered photos of babies, relatives, and children, and you would know I value a strong family life. All manner of Legos and castles under construction would speak of the "creative disorder" rampant in our home. A hint of doggy odor in the entryway would alert you to the presence of our beloved (but ill-mannered) Frances the Mutt. You'd know the books we're currently reading, because you'd find them in the bathroom. Very quickly you'd discover that we postpone fixing things, that I love garage-sale finds, and that a picture of a laughing Christ hangs prominently over the whole enterprise. "Welcome to my place" are words that invite intimacy, and I speak them now far more easily after experiencing loving hospitality myself.

What about entertaining? What do we do with folks once we've welcomed them in? Publius entertained Paul and his fellow travelers for three days. Do you suppose they visited every tourist spot on the island and shopped the tucked-away boutiques? Hardly. Paul realized very quickly that he'd been welcomed into the house even though Publius's father "was sick in bed, suffering from fever and dysentery" (Acts 28:8). Paul responded to this difficult situation with compassion and prayed for him, placing his hands right on the sick man. Now that's an interesting concept of entertainment! Sometimes we think of entertaining as creating a sparkling agenda for our guests; we feel compelled to spotlight our own strengths. But at the core of hospitable entertaining lies a willingness to share both the joys and heartaches of life. Who has time to sterilize life into some sort of antiseptic condition in order to entertain? Make your guests part of the family, and they will truly feel at home.

But let's be honest. The biggest hitch in showing hospitality is lack of time. Each day has too few hours to get basic life maintenance done, much less reach out to someone else. It's reassuring to remember that we are not the Messiah—Jesus is! If we regularly spend time with the Lord so we are restored in body, mind, and spirit, then reaching out will be much more joyful.

Remember, too, that hospitality giving has its seasons. A friend once attended a talk by a woman known for her welcoming heart and open home. After listening to the speaker urge involvement in caring for those in pain, my friend asked, "How do I begin to open my home? I have three small children, and I'm overwhelmed most of the time."

"Oh, my dear," said the speaker. "Your home is open exactly the way it needs to be right now—to a husband and three tiny children who need your full attention. There will come another season in your life, and then you'll be able to reach out differently!"

The body of Christ is meant to function as a healthy unit, taking into account the seasons, gifts, and limitations of each member. Pooling our resources with other members of the body means we can be hospitable far beyond our own abilities. My experience with British hospitality taught my individualistic, "I can do it myself" mind-set a lesson about the body of Christ. A church filled with hospitality-givers can be a potent force for Christ and a guard against individual burnout. Even as I write today, our local church is hosting a group of ten students from a former Eastern bloc country for a month. Though our family is unable to house a student this time, I watch with joy as other Christians open their homes. These ten men and women will return to their uncertain and emerging homeland having experienced the love of Christ in meals lovingly served, transportation graciously given, and lives openly shared. What an opportunity we have to affect the shrinking world through the corporate hospitality we give as a church!

The 1990s present a dizzying array of options. But the ministry of welcoming others into our homes and lives remains a call we must not ignore. No matter the season of life or the limitations of schedule, we can ask the Lord for a heart that's open and the eyes to see those who crave a resting place.

Memorable Holiday Visitors

Ideas for Quick-'n'-Easy Entertaining

Great Party Themes

_____

Making the Untraditional Traditional

If your holiday routine has changed over the years due to adding extended family, losing a loved one, or not being able to travel or do "traditional things," maybe it's time to make the "untraditional" traditional. What family celebrations are unique? Try making those a new tradition. If you're "tired of the same old thing," remember: All traditions are just waiting to be started by someone, and maybe that someone is you!

The first Christmas our small extended family spent around the candles and carved turkey of a restaurant, I ached for the familiarity of holidays spent around Grandma's giant dining-room table. But Grandma's home was no longer hers, and our dwindling family had scattered across several states. This new setting—at first so "untraditional"—now has become our family's holiday gathering place. Granted, it will never be the same as the Christmases of my past. But its unfamiliarity has given way to a specialness all its own.

JANE JOHNSON STRUCK

Center Christmas on Christ

F. EVELYN BENCE

No matter what your pre-Christmas festivities—church socials, office parties, grab-bag exchanges, school concerts, shopping sprees—make this year's December 25 a day especially set apart as Christ's.

As soon as you get up in the morning, turn on religious carols and play them all day. In many areas such programming is available on a religious or classical radio station. Check newspaper listings ahead of time or call a few stations that seem most likely to feature special holiday programs. If the radio can't meet your needs, gather up a few records or tapes and wear them thin. (If you've already played your albums until you're sick of them, freshen up your selection by arranging a Christmas-Eve trade with another household.)

Go to church. If your church doesn't have a service, locate one that does. Many ethnic congregations and liturgical churches place emphasis on Christmas worship. Although the service may not be the kind you're used to, center your thoughts on the Christ child, whose birth you are celebrating.

If "real" church seems out of the question, have a service at home. Structure a family worship time that involves more than a quick reading through Luke's account. You might ask that the family come prepared to praise God as each person sees fit—by requesting a favorite "congregational" carol, by playing an instrumental solo, by reading a story or poem, by praying, and so forth.

A week before Christmas, ask that all family members wrap up something they would have given to Jesus if they had been at the manger. Make it clear they shouldn't go buy an item; rather, their gift should be something already in their possession or gathered from nature. Place the packages in a specific corner under the tree and, as part of your gift opening or at another designated part of Christmas Day, have each person unwrap another's gift on behalf of the Christ child. If it seems appropriate, the giver might explain why he or she chose a particular present.

GETTING HER GOAT

My three-year-old son, Grant, told me he learned a new song in children's church about goats on the mountain when Jesus was born. I hadn't heard that one before, so I asked him to sing it. He began, "Goats tell it on the mountain, over the hills and everywhere. Goats tell it on the mountain, that Jesus Christ is born."

DEBBIE HARMON

Quick 'n' Easy Holiday Favorites

MARSHA CROCKETT

Whether our dream holiday is filled with Victorian lace or simple country traditions, what we usually end up with are frazzled nerves. But don't despair! There's hope for filling the season with old-fashioned fun in half the time and effort your grandmother needed. Sample these modern renditions of some old Christmas traditions.

Christmas Cookies
What's so charming about mixing, baking, and cleaning? The real fun comes from creating, decorating, and sharing the finished product with the family. Take work out of cookie making by using premixed dough. Or buy plain sugar cookies and use canned icing and candy to decorate. The kids will be just as proud of their creations as you are of your still-clean kitchen.

Wassail Bowl
This old-fashioned drink can be whipped up in minutes and left to brew in the crockpot. Use apple cider and add your own cloves and cinnamon sticks. Or use packaged spiced cider mix. The cider can be kept warm for hours, always ready for unexpected company or chilly carolers.

Gingerbread Houses
This most tedious task can be turned into fun for the whole family when the houses are built with graham crackers, ready-made icing, and Christmas candy. "Glue" the edges of crackers together with icing. Then "paint" the house with leftover icing and add candy-coated shingles, windows, and doors.

Homemade Garland
Anyone who has tried knows the hours involved to string a garland large enough to encircle even a small tree. Instead, try using popcorn and cranberry miniwreaths to hang on the tree. Simply cut a 12-inch thread or thin wire to string the goodies, leaving enough room to knot ends together. Then tie it all up in ribbon and lace.

The Oldest Tradition

Homespun traditions are only a nice touch to the oldest tradition of all—remembering the Christ child. Revive this most meaningful part of Christmas by reading the Christmas story, taking the children to a live nativity scene, or baking a birthday cake and singing "Happy Birthday" to Jesus.

"I said big, but not that big!"

Traditions WITH A TWIST

Ever since I can remember, Mom would place under the tree for my two sisters and me three presents with tags that read, "Open Christmas Eve." After we ate supper and took our baths, we each grabbed our present and eagerly opened it. Inside we always found brand-new pajamas! We'd hurry to put them on, jump into bed, and try to sleep on what seemed the longest night of the year.

Well, thirty years later, the tradition continues. Whether or not we're all together, my mother, my sisters, and our children eagerly look through the presents and grab the ones marked "Open Christmas Eve." Once again we put on new pajamas and try to get through what still seems to be the longest night of the year!

CINDY MONTOYA

Alone for the Holidays

KAREN HEFFNER

Maybe you've lost your spouse this year to death or divorce. Or you've just been transferred, and you'll be away from family over the holidays. Or you're single and have decided not to go to your parents' home this year. Everyone else seems to be looking forward to the coming season, but you have mixed feelings. Here are some tips for coping when you're alone:

Maintain at least a few family traditions. If grown children and grandchildren always gathered at your home on Thanksgiving or Christmas Eve, or if the neighbors always joined you for carols and cider, invite them again this year, if possible. Make it simple, but *do* get together.

Look for special holiday events in your community and invite another person (or family member) who is alone to join you. Concerts, school and church programs, or a visit to a special light display cost little but give much pleasure.

Reach out. Help a community agency deliver food baskets, or help an elderly friend address her cards. Lend your help in sewing costumes or making sets for the children's program at church. Volunteering can open doors for new friendships and continued service long after the holidays.

Accept social invitations whenever possible, and issue a few yourself. Although it can be unsettling to attend a party alone when you were once part of a couple, it's important not to sever old friendships or refuse to build new ones.

Do something new. Keep a journal or begin writing poetry. Enroll in a class, start a new hobby, or renew an old one. Go to the library every week for a fresh supply of books or recordings.

Allow for extra rest. Fatigue magnifies depression. Take time to read, meditate, and talk to a good friend about how you're feeling. Allow yourself to cry. (If depression is severe or persists, seek professional help from a counselor or spiritual advisor.)

Be kind to yourself. Remember, God has promised to give comfort to those who come to him.

ALL IS CALM

As our family was eating dinner one evening before Advent began, I asked, "Who can tell me what the four candles in the Advent wreath represent?" Luke, my seven year old, exuberantly began, "There's love, joy, peace, and . . . and . . ." Eager to keep up with her brother, six-year-old Elise excitedly broke in, "I know! Peace and quiet!"

MICHELE HARDIE

What about Hanukkah?

KATHY BENCE

About the time Christians are anticipating the coming of Christmas, their Jewish friends are celebrating another religious holiday—Hanukkah.

Hanukkah, otherwise called the Feast of Lights, literally means "dedication." To devout Jews, it's a minor holiday that commemorates the purification of the temple after the Abomination of Desolation in 164 B.C. Antiochus Epiphanes had desecrated the temple by slaughtering a pig upon its altar.

The Jews, outraged at such an act, looked for a way to purify the temple. As the legend tells it, they found a cruse of oil in the temple, enough to last for a day. Miraculously, it lasted eight days. Today, Jews remember this miracle during Hanukkah by lighting one candle each day on an eight-pronged candlestick called a menorah.

How should Christians regard the Jewish Feast of Lights? Here are several tips from Jewish friends:

1. Realize that Jews do not celebrate Hanukkah as we do Christmas. Gifts are not the main focus of their celebration and are usually given only to children to offset the commercialism of Christmas.

2. Jewish people usually do not have a Christmas tree and may not be interested in attending a tree-trimming party. While a tree is not distinctly religious, to Jews it means Christmas.

3. It will mean a lot to a Jewish friend if you learn what Hanukkah means and are conversant on the subject.

4. Do not elevate Hanukkah to extreme significance. It remains a minor holiday. Devout Jews' high holy days are Yom Kippur and Rosh Hashanah.

5. Ask a Jewish friend to allow you to take part in his or her family's Hanukkah celebration.

Remember that the holiday is a symbol of the Jews' steadfast faith under oppression—a quality we all desire.

Traditions WITH A TWIST

Every Christmas Eve, our family dresses up in old bathrobes, sheets, and whatever else we can find and acts out the story of Christ's birth—complete with stuffed tigers, poodles, and lambs for the animals. The youngest child gets to be baby Jesus.

Each year we take a group photo, laugh hysterically over everyone's creative outfits, and share—as a family—in the joy and wonder of Jesus' birth.

EVANGELINE CRAMER

Family Stories

EILEEN SILVA KINDIG

Several Christmases ago, my oldest daughter, Moira, received a tape recorder. Anxious to try it out, she began "interviewing" various relatives at our holiday gathering. Not finding too many willing subjects, she finally settled on my husband's ninety-year-old great-aunt Peg. Tickled to be the center of attention, this usually quiet woman filled both sides of a sixty-minute tape with stories of her childhood along the riverfront in Marietta, Ohio. As she wove together tales of old-fashioned church suppers, moving to a new house, and surviving the Great Flood of 1913, our family abandoned the dessert table to listen spellbound to her stories.

What happened in our living room that day was more than just a pleasant diversion—it was a communion of family. By sharing her stories, Aunt Peg reached across the generations and gave us a rare gift—a glimpse of our family heritage. Aunt Peg's simple faith in God's goodness throughout her long life left an indelible mark on our hearts. Our family felt connected in a deeper way.

Everyone—from sociologists to politicians—bemoans the breakdown of the American family. While storytelling is by no means a cure, telling family stories can strengthen your family's bond by nurturing your family's uniqueness. When you tell a story about your child's birth, laugh together about the crazy vacation you took to Yellowstone, or tell your kids about how their great-grandparents came to America, you can't help but express the love and pride you feel for your family. Family stories foster intimacy and a sense of real belonging.

But family stories serve yet a deeper purpose. According to psychologist Jerome Singer, preschoolers watch an average of twenty-one hours a week of television, while older children log a whopping thirty-five hours. Unfortunately, many of today's most crucial lessons about life are being taught by the Simpsons and the Teenage Mutant Ninja Turtles! Let's let the wisdom of parents and grandparents take the spotlight for a change.

Just as Jesus used parables to imprint spiritual truths on the minds of his followers, parents, too, can use stories to teach their kids important truths. Whether you're the first in the family to become a believer or whether your family's commitment to Christ spans many generations, your children can learn much about walking with God by hearing you tell about *your* walk or the way their ancestors trusted in him.

The truth is, the busier our families get, the more we need stories to anchor us to our roots, our faith, and each other. The beauty of storytelling is that it can happen anytime you're together—while you're driving in the car, decorating your Christmas tree, or eating cheeseburgers at the local fast-food restaurant. You can make it part of your children's bedtime routine or the centerpiece of a reunion. The when or where isn't important. What matters is that *everyone*—from the youngest to the oldest—be involved.

If such a tradition has never played a significant role in your family life, it's not too late to get started. Here are some tips to help:

Talk about how God has worked in your life. Stories that show how God has blessed your family offer your children a more deeply intimate look at spirituality.

My husband and I tell stories about the events that led to the adoption of each of our daughters, because we believe God chose them especially for our family.

"Tell me about when I came from Korea," Caitie will implore. "And don't forget the part about how you had to wait so long to get me!"

At seventeen, our oldest daughter, Moira, rolls her eyes and moans, "Here we go *again!*" every time I launch into a story about her childhood. But she can't quite hide the smile that plays on her lips when I recount the joy we felt when we first saw her or how thankful I was the day she fell down the basement stairs on her first birthday and landed safely in a pail at the bottom.

We also tell our girls stories about their adoptive grandparents' immigration—how God blessed and protected them in a new land. And we freely talk about the present, how God continues to guide us through the aftermath of a recent family business crisis. What a powerful ongoing reminder of God's faithfulness these stories are to us!

Crack open the family album. Old snapshots make a great starting point for story ideas. In addition to reminiscing over your own family photos, ask your parents to share pictures and/or home movies from their childhoods or the years when they were raising you. Children love to see Mom and Dad or Grandma and Grandpa when they were kids and hear about their adventures.

This type of storytelling also lets kids in on the secret that their parents weren't always "perfect"—that they, too, experienced doubts, fears, and problems.

I recently discovered this firsthand when my eight-year-old daughter, Caitie, became upset about a funeral scene she had seen in a movie she'd watched at a friend's house.

"I'm scared, Mommy," she whispered as she told me about the movie. "I'm afraid God will make me or somebody else in our family dead."

Instantly her fear transported me back thirty years to the day I attended an infant's funeral. By telling her that story in precise detail—how I felt, what I thought—Caitie knew I understood her fears and we were able to explore deep feelings about life and death that otherwise might not have surfaced.

Make storytelling an event. "Whenever our family starts telling stories, Mom *always* makes hot chocolate!" a friend's eight-year-old son told me.

Families who have made storytelling a tradition understand that *who* tells the story becomes as important as the stories themselves. Certain stories "belong" to certain people. Even complaints—such as my daughter's "Here we go *again!*"—become part of the expected routine.

Encourage all family members to participate. When storytelling moves into high gear, it requires audience participation. Even preschoolers can be encouraged to tell stories. Let them tell an event from their day at play group or Sunday school. Listen carefully and ask questions to show your interest. Often their stories give great insight into how they view their world—and sometimes become part of family legend!

Last summer, my friend Connie asked her five-year-old daughter to recount the family vacation.

"Well," Stephanie said dramatically, "we drove and drove and finally we came to the troll bridge."

"*What* kind of bridge?" Connie asked.

"The troll bridge," Stephanie replied patiently. "You know, where you have to pay money. We didn't see the trolls though, because it was daytime and there was just a lady there."

This summer the family vacationed again—of course stopping at the "troll bridge!"

Don't skimp on the details. Don't just say, "The dog we had back then." Say, "The brown sheepdog we called Dusty because Grandma always said he looked like a mop." Vivid descriptions—the sound of the wind, the colors of the sky—are the enchanting elements that draw your listeners in.

As a child, I spent many evenings in the back parlor of my grandmother's house, listening to her tell stories about her childhood in Ireland. Even now I remember the snatches of songs she sang, feel her freckled arms around me, and see the moonlight falling softly over her old treadle sewing machine by the window. Because of these stories, I have carried her close to me all of my life, even though she died the Christmas I was nineteen.

Refrain from interpreting. This is tricky, since we all tend to want to tack a moral onto the end of a story. But don't! The whole idea of storytelling is for the listener to draw his or her own conclusions. Children take from a story what they need at the time. That's why repetition is wonderful. The next time they hear the same story, they may absorb it on an entirely different level.

Don't be afraid of stories that are hard to tell. Sometimes crisis stories—about the death of a loved one or some other emotionally difficult circumstance—and stories of miracles, near-misses, and God's loving protection throughout the generations provide balm for the spirit and strengthen our faith. When children experience God's love and faithfulness working through people they know and love, the lesson learned is unforgettable.

Family stories—no matter how small or seemingly insignificant—tell us who we are and how we're irrevocably connected. They're part of an oral tradition that reaches back into biblical times. If we are to celebrate fully the joy of family, then we must value our stories as greatly as the family photo album or Grandmother's heirloom china. With care, the special stories of your family will last longer than a lifetime.

MOO TESTAMENT

While helping my five-year-old twins rehearse "Away in a Manger" for their Christmas concert, I struggled to explain the lyrics "the cattle are lowing." When I told them that people spoke differently in Old Testament times than they do today, my daughter, Robin, piped up, "Old Testament cows low—and New Testament cows moo!"

KATHIE ERWIN

"I didn't see anything I liked. . . . Do you have anything else?"

Traditions WITH A TWIST

About a week before Christmas, our family of seven writes on separate slips of paper the special "gift" we'd like to give God in the coming year. These gifts range from having a quieter spirit to telling Jesus "I love you" every day. Our older kids help the younger ones write what they want to give. Then we put the slips of paper into a box, wrap it, label it "To Jesus," and put it under our tree.

On Christmas Day, we open the package for Jesus first and read out loud everyone's "gift." Then we read the original Christmas story in the Gospel of Luke and pray to commit our ways to God. After dinner, we have birthday cake and sing "Happy Birthday" to Jesus. That song never sounds as sweet as it does on Christmas!

PAMELA ARIAS

"I figure as it burns down, we'll keep shoving it in."

The Ever-Ready Christmas Tree

Liz Curtis Higgs

In our family, each Christmas is defined by one specific memory—the Christmas I made smoked turkey without meaning to, the year I gave everyone gifts in brown paper bags, the Christmas Day we spent on the Pennsylvania Turnpike. But 1992 will always be remembered as the year I received a ten-foot artificial Christmas tree—decorated from top to bottom—as an honorarium for speaking for a local charitable organization. Usually we make a trip to a nearby tree farm and cut down our own fragrant spruce, but we were in the process of moving, so a ready-to-go tree was a welcome gift.

One afternoon, early that December, while I was in the middle of painting the dining-room ceiling in our new home, the phone call came: "Mrs. Higgs, we're ready to deliver your tree."

"Great!" I said, my voice bouncing off the bare walls. "How about next Wednesday around three o'clock?"

The caller was silent for a moment, then said, "Uh, Mrs. Higgs, I'm calling you from a car phone. We're a block away from your house."

"Are you kidding?" I exclaimed, backing down the ladder. They were not. Minutes later, a delivery truck pulled into our drive. As I hurried out to direct traffic, the tree was unloaded, shrouded in plastic wrap. It was enormous.

"Where do you want it?" was their logical question.

"Let's just put it in the garage for now," I suggested, pointing the way.

Two fullback-size fellas grunted and sweated as they dragged our tree toward the garage. *Gee,* I thought, *it sure looks heavy.* Finally, they gave the tree a mighty yank, and the ornamental giant landed just inside the garage door.

Nearly a week passed, and our house was beginning to look like home. "It's probably about time we bring in the Christmas tree," I casually mentioned to my husband, Bill, one evening. He looked puzzled. "What tree?" he asked.

"Remember that free tree I was given? It's just inside the garage door. C'mon, I'll hold the door and you can carry it in."

Shaking his head, Bill pulled on his coat and headed out into the night. The garage door swooshed open, and then I heard a distinct groan—"Liz-z-zz!" I grabbed my own coat and made tracks for the garage.

It was not a pretty sight. Cinnamon sticks, once neatly tied with bright-red ribbons on the tree, dangled forlornly, having served as a holiday lunch for some hungry squirrels that had chewed through the plastic wrap. A stray cat had celebrated the season by knocking off mice-sized ornaments that had rolled from one end of our garage to another. The angel perching on the ten-foot tree top drooped sideways, obviously ashamed of what had transpired below.

"Oh, Bill!" I moaned, my eyes stinging with tears. "Is it hopeless?"

"Well, it'll take some effort to make the tree look nice again," he said, picking up a glass ball that had survived the cat-astrophe.

"No problem," I assured him. "I found a box of ornaments yesterday, so we'll have plenty to work with. Think you can carry it in?"

What man in his macho mind would say, "No, it's too heavy for me"? Bill was no exception. He valiantly bent down, grabbed it at the base, and pulled. It moved a fraction of an inch. Another pull yielded almost an inch. Progress. Two more yanks brought it another two inches further along. Bill straightened up. "Did one man move this in here?" he asked, wiping his brow.

"No, two men," I answered reluctantly. "Big guys." Bill was not comforted by this news. "I can help," I offered, grabbing the trunk midway up. "You take the bottom, and I'll take the top." Which is exactly what I did. Took the top right off the tree.

Never having owned an artificial tree, I didn't know they came apart. You haven't lived till you've tried to steer five feet of heavily decorated Christmas tree back into an opening the size of a pencil. With one hand. And with one husband jumping up and down, shouting instructions. It got very old, very fast.

"Here, you try it!" I said, exasperated, giving him room to reach through the prickly branches and grab hold of the trunk. Between us, we managed to get the tree back together. Above us, even the angel looked grateful. "OK," I said, standing back, "there must be a better way."

Scooting some discarded cardboard under the tree, we finally were able to drag it through the door and onto the driveway. It took us fifteen minutes to move it all of three feet. I looked up to see two noses pressed against the kitchen window as our children watched us move the tree down the driveway, then across the front yard. Had a camera been handy to capture the moment, you would have seen Bill and a Christmas tree lying across his back, me hanging on to the base for dear life, going backward up the (thankfully) short flight of steps to our front porch.

A new problem became immediately apparent: Our ten-foot tree was four-feet wide with ornaments; our eight-foot front door was three-feet wide with hinges. "We go in backward," Bill announced. I winced as the sound of breaking glass and squishing cranberries greeted our ears.

"Pull in your tummy!" I shouted to the tree as a final heave-ho brought it suddenly into the foyer of our old farmhouse.

Bill dropped to the foot of the steps, as the kids danced around in excitement. "OK," he said wearily, "where do you want it?"

My mind went blank. "I haven't the faintest idea," I finally confessed, looking down the hall and through the doorways around us. "There are boxes in every single room except the kitchen. It's big enough, I guess. Want to drag it there?"

The hall rug was a big help as we headed east. Two more doorways dislodged a few more ornaments, but soon the tree stood more or less straight in the exact center of the kitchen. The angel now soared above the ceiling fan, and I cautioned the kids that under no circumstances was the fan to be turned on.

After hustling our wide-eyed elves off to bed, Bill and I spent an hour whipping the tree into shape. The damage wasn't as bad as we had feared, and once the broken decorations were replaced with some old favorites, the tree looked spiffy again. Relieved that we had accomplished our task, we crawled off to bed.

The Christmas tree spent several days in our kitchen. At first, every time I came around the corner, I jumped back at the sight of it standing there, quietly taking up half the room. But as Christmas grew closer, we grew accustomed to the green giant in the kitchen and acted surprised when friends walked in and did a double take.

"What is that?" they would say.

"A Christmas tree, of course," we would answer. "Don't you have one?"

But finally, it became unhandy to have it in the center of the busiest room in the house, so we looked for a new location. "There are fewer boxes in the downstairs bedroom," I suggested. "How 'bout there?" Another two doorways to maneuver, and the tree had a new venue. Now when friends asked us if we still had a Christmas tree in our kitchen, we smiled brightly and said, "Oh, no! It's in the front bedroom."

A few days later, however, the tree was transported to the family room while I finished decorating the bedroom for guests. That move involved going down a step, plus avoiding a ceiling fan that was accidentally activated. But the tree showed great staying power. The only room on the first floor it didn't visit was the bathroom—but that was only because of logistics.

By Christmas Eve, it had found its final resting place—the dining room. A bit worse for wear but still a glorious sight, it fit perfectly in the corner. We hadn't lost a single twinkling bulb in all the hauling around, and the angel stood proudly at the helm, looking up at a freshly painted ceiling just inches above her halo.

When Bill's parents and grandmother arrived for our traditional bowl of homemade soup and bread, we hurried them in to see our tree. "It's lovely!" my mother-in-law exclaimed.

"It was free," my son Matthew declared proudly. Like his father, he appreciated a good bargain.

Three-year-old Lillian, her eyes full of wonder, said, "Our tree has lived in every room, but this is her favorite!"

My in-laws looked at me for an explanation, but I just smiled.

"That's true," I said. "Some trees are pickier than others."

Our first Christmas in our new home went without a hitch. When New Year's Day arrived—traditionally the day for taking down a cut Christmas tree and sweeping up the dried needles—I had a sudden burst of inspiration: This tree would never lose its needles. I could enjoy it right through Epiphany!

By mid-January, still cozy in its corner of the dining room, the tree continued to look fresh and green—though a tad off-season. I removed all the yuletide ornaments and left only the twinkling lights and white snowflakes on its branches. "It's a January tree," I informed the family, and there the tree stayed.

When February came along, it seemed appropriate to replace the snowflakes with valentines, so the kids and I had a ball covering the tree with paper hearts. *Not every family has a valentine tree,* I thought warmly.

Frankly, the shamrocks in March got lost amidst all the green, so on the first of April, we moved quickly to Easter eggs of every hue and multicolored grass dripping from the branches. It was my favorite month so far.

Friends were less impressed. When my in-laws came for Easter dinner, they took one look and said, "Well!"

By May, it was getting harder to keep the branches dust free, and, though lovely, sunflowers couldn't overcome the Christmas-in-July look. Visitors rolled their eyes, and even the kids wearied of explaining to people that "Mom thought it would be fun to have a holiday tree all year."

By August, the tree was history—a two-piece memory shoved back in the corner of the garage, where it all began.

November rolled around, and it was time for my annual holiday presentation for that charitable organization. With their request for my speaking services came their generous offer: "Liz, may we give you another tree this year?"

"No thanks," I said. "I'll take a wreath."

A Date with My Calendar

KAREN HEFFNER

My annual rite of the "Changing of the Calendar" begins on an early November morning.

As other shoppers clog the stationery store aisles in front of Christmas cards and gift wraps, I pick my way to the party supplies in eager anticipation. I find the calendar carousel, then nudge it gently, setting into motion a lovely panorama of colors and forms—fresh calendars twirling like ballerinas on opening night.

Choosing is never easy. My new calendar must be aesthetically pleasing, for it must command my attention for the next twelve months (if only an involuntary glance as I answer the telephone next to it). And it must be practical, with ample squares and margins for writing.

I settle on a calendar that depicts the industrious woman described in Proverbs 31. Dressed in jeans and a sweatshirt, with short curly hair and oversized pink-rimmed glasses (not unlike myself), the calendar lady is busy at the tasks for which she is commended. The good woman makes me laugh, confirming my choice. A calendar must never be too serious.

But the "Changing of the Calendar" is fully accomplished only when two distinct processes are complete. The first involves making those initial marks in my new calendar's pristine squares. Carefully I transcribe birthdays and anniversaries, all the while reminded of the richness family and friends bring to my life. *What will the new year hold for each of us?* I wonder.

The second process takes much longer. I am compelled, it seems, to sit down with a cup of coffee and leisurely read the outdated calendar as I might read a diary. Our family life is chronicled in my collection of calendars, and when I finish reviewing this year's model, it will join its predecessors in "the archives," the gray metal filing cabinet that holds our memories. I have them all—from the time my baby was two.

As I leaf through their pages, images invade my mind: the tiny, turned-in feet, later encased in casts; the stitches that resulted when a small forehead did battle with the piano bench; the trauma of stubborn acne and frightening asthma attacks; the broken toe suffered in a collision with a door frame while trying to outrun a sister to the ringing telephone. The number of our doctor trips seems incredibly high—but calendars don't lie about such things.

My calendars also give mute testimony to life's joyous events, to experiences that even now produce a lump in my throat. The birth of a grandchild appears on the same page as the death of a beloved grandmother; the tiny child, her great-great-grandma's namesake, was publicly dedicated to Jesus on the very day the frail ninety-eight-year-old saw him face-to-face. I am reminded anew of God's faithfulness from generation to generation. Birthdays, weddings, anniversaries—all are occasions that call for a celebration of life and love, and all are a reflection of the struggles and victories that are an inescapable part of life.

The words of the old hymn spring unbidden to mind: "O God, our help in ages past, our hope for years to come." Years pass and new adventures are heralded—my calendar records them all. Held lightly in my hands, they seem almost alive, able to evoke the laughter and tears that inevitably accompany nostalgic journeys.

Someday I may have a journal—the one I'm always intending to start. But until then, I have my calendars—and that is good enough for me.

Celebrating Christmas Eve

Christmas Morning Traditions

_____
_____
_____
_____
_____
_____
_____
_____
_____
_____
_____
_____
_____
_____
_____
_____
_____
_____
_____
_____
_____
_____
_____
_____
_____
_____
_____

Other "Traditions with a Twist"

_____

_____

_____

_____

_____

_____

_____

_____

_____

_____

_____

_____

_____

_____

_____

_____

_____

_____

_____

_____

_____

_____

_____

_____

_____

_____

_____

Restoring the Joy
and Meaning
of Christmas

❦ ❦ ❦

"Joy to the world! the Lord is come. Let earth
receive her King!" These words express so
joyfully what Christ's coming as a
flesh-and-blood baby in the manger should
mean to us. But sometimes that joy can be
swallowed up by the flurry of activity
surrounding the holidays. This Christmas let
us choose to celebrate God, who made the
event possible—and changed our lives forever
in the process, giving us eternal hope and joy.

Joy is the greatest living testimony for a Christian.
How can you be a testimony if your life is without joy?

MARILYN QUAYLE

Hope for the Holiday Weary

DEBBIE L. BARKER

It was Christmas—my seventeenth—when it all began. Holiday weariness, that is. As I sat Indian-style before Grandma's hearth, surrounded by my laughing, package-opening family, I suddenly felt drained. At first I wrote it off to fatigue from all the holiday preparations. Then I realized my fatigue really masked a sadness over our futile attempts to buy real, lasting joy. With each holiday that followed, I continued to feel weary. After years of pondering why I felt this way during the holidays, I arrived at a plausible explanation. My family tended to celebrate the *event* instead of celebrating God, who made the event possible.

It's an easy snare to fall into. Misconceived desires and unrealistic expectations, fueled by materialism and what author C. S. Lewis once called the "tyranny of ought," can deny any sense of joy in celebration.

Lewis was writing about Christmas *ought*. But his thoughts apply to any occasion. For example: Carol bought a card for my birthday, so I *ought* to get her one. Sister Sue sent gifts on Mother's and Father's Days, so I *ought* to do

something for their anniversary. Mother always kept her house spotless, so I *ought* to do the white-glove test before friends arrive at my house for Thanksgiving. When we have these expectations, it's no wonder so many of us suffer weariness.

So where's the hope? I'm discovering that when my family and I actively praise and worship our Lord, traditional celebrations sparkle. Our activities and giving are more creative, and my weariness disappears as we rejoice over the Lord's working in our lives.

Below are some adjustments we've made to family celebrations that have opened the door to hope-filled joy.

Practice hospitality rather than entertaining. When my husband, David, and I lived in our first home, I was reluctant to invite his parents, grandparents, and two brothers for a birthday party. Our house and furniture collection were so small several of us would have to sit on the floor. "How can we have a party when there aren't enough chairs for everyone?" I groaned. We managed, and no one seemed worse for the experience.

Since those days, I no longer "entertain" in my home. Instead, I practice a hospitality that allows me the freedom to tell my guests, "Pull up a piece of floor and have a seat." It's OK for my house and preparations to be less than perfect if my guests know they're welcomed and loved.

Open celebrations to those outside the family circle. Last Thanksgiving was to be a reunion celebration marking the end of a painful separation within my sister's family. More than any time past, I wanted that celebration day kept private. It was not to be. David asked permission to invite another family to join us—a family that was having its own tough time holding together.

After my initial veto, the Holy Spirit reminded me of how others had recently taken in my sister and members of her family during a difficult time. How could we do less? Our friends joined us and enjoyed a day that I hope helped lighten their burden. I realized the Lord's plans for our day were not my plans. The Lord truly adds joy to celebrations shared with the hurting.

Pray and plan for holiday celebrations and gift giving. I usually don't think about a holiday until the last minute— then I feel pressured by guilt. However, one Christmas stands out

as a partial victory. The newspaper's Christmas-shopping countdown informed me I had fourteen days left when I decided to pray about each gift. Two days before Christmas, I still had one gift to buy—an unknown something for Dad.

I didn't have any idea what he needed, but the Holy Spirit did. When I walked into the first department store on my final shopping trip, I immediately found a charcoal gray, medium-weight sweater, perfect in every way. The sweater has remained a favorite of my dad's—a reminder to me that God answers even our little prayers.

Give gifts that celebrate memories. Early in our marriage, my husband's grandma Keith gave me an afghan I'd watched her start when Grandpa Keith was in surgery. The afghan had eased our waiting-room anxiety—providing fuel for conversation as I admired it and reason for laughter as I clumsily attempted to crochet with Grandma.

What makes this afghan such a treasured gift—even more than the special memories of getting to know Grandma better—is its constant reminder of how God preserved Grandpa, a precious member of our family's celebration circle.

Establish a firm holiday budget. Several years ago, David and I cut up our credit cards, committing to cash-only buying and firm budgeting. We set our Christmas budget, assigned per-person dollar limits, and sallied forth to "buy Christmas." We were astonished at the impossibility of our task. What we then considered meaningful gifts far exceeded our budget.

Since then we've redefined "meaningful gifts." David and I discovered help-gifts after my dad became unable to do many of his favorite—and not-so-favorite—tasks around the house. We've spent up to a week at home helping Mom and Dad with everything from figuring taxes to putting up drywall.

Combining help-gifts and homemade treasures with store-bought items enabled us to stay within our budget, feeling confident of each gift's appropriateness.

Give a cup of cold water. The most meaningful element of my last Christmas celebration was participating, for the first time, in a tradition my sister began when her children were small. We located a young family, each member of which was handicapped and the parents unemployed. On Christmas Eve we took them dinner, household maintenance items, and something special for each individual—and gave them Christmas in the name of Jesus.

I learned it *is* possible to touch strangers' lives with tangible expressions of Christ's love. I discovered a joy in giving that I missed when I simply donated money to a relief organization.

Make your celebrations holy. Once I realized my need for individuality, I started looking for a holiday to make my own. For me, Easter is an intensely personal and holy holiday. It's also a time I particularly desire to share my devotion to my Savior.

This year, I broke from all past family traditions and initiated my own. I brought together my siblings and their families for a Maundy Thursday celebration. We gathered by family units around the dinner table where we prayed, read Scripture, and celebrated our Lord's Last Supper. Each family shared a common cup and passed the bread around the table. We all shared in the awe and appreciation of Jesus' sacrifice as we discussed the meaning of what he did for us and the scriptural elements of the traditional Passover celebration. Dinner completed, we listened to a poetic monologue on Christ's crucifixion, prayed, and then went our own ways to anticipate his resurrection.

On Easter morning, David and I went alone up the hill behind our home. We took with us praise music, a Bible, hearts ready to pray, and our breakfast. From our sunny hilltop perch, we praised our risen Savior and prayed for our neighbors, friends, family, and nation.

While we did this instead of a formal church service, I still believe corporate worship is important. However, for us, at the time, that was a holy day—not merely a holiday.

Practice thanking God, making him the center of all celebration. Until recently, I'd never considered thanksgiving as integral to any holiday other than *Thanksgiving.* Now I'm seeing that all holidays are times to thank God for the good gifts he constantly gives us.

When my grandmother died on my last birthday, I was grieved by her passing, but the Holy Spirit opened my eyes to see through my grief. I was thankful for his presence and acknowledged his great mercy in giving, preserving, and even taking life. A more thankful heart was the Lord's birthday gift to me.

I finally understood what I'd been seeking all those years. I want all holidays to be holy days, times of thanksgiving to God for each member of our family and for what he's doing in and through their lives. I want our focus to be on God and allow the other elements of celebration to be the overflow of hearts filled with him. There's no way to *buy* that kind of celebration.

Following my last birthday, I made a resolution: no more holiday weariness anchored by ought-to's—only hope anchored by thanksgiving and love. Happy holidays—all of them!

Did $omebody $ay Chri$tma$?

JEANNE ZORNES

Overspending is one holiday tradition we'd all like to avoid. Follow these tips to cut down on Christmas budget-busters.

1. Wrap gifts in white tissue, comics, or squares of Christmas fabric (bought at drastic discounts in off-season). Tie with yarn.

2. Buy pumpkins after Halloween when they're cheap. Bake, save the pulp, then devote a day to making pumpkin bread to freeze ahead for gifts.

3. If family gift exchanges have gotten out of hand, discuss drawing names and setting a lower price limit, such as ten dollars.

4. Are Christmas trees too expensive where you live? Make a majestic poinsettia your "tree." If you miss the tree fragrance, get a pine-scented candle.

5. Save shortening cans, decorate with adhesive paper, then fill with homemade granola or add-water-only cocoa mix ($2\frac{3}{4}$ cup commercial chocolate drink mix plus 7 cups dry milk—use scant $\frac{1}{4}$ cup per serving).

6. Staple promises to a new calendar, such as "January—go sledding as a family" or "April—a clean garage, guaranteed!" or "August—family campout in the backyard."

7. Offer gifts of service: organizing food coupons, canning during harvest, weeding flower gardens once, painting a piece of furniture, watching children for an afternoon, promising to vacuum the car once a week, etc. Write the "gift-promise" on a homemade card.

8. Skip-sending Christmas cards. Instead, take time during the January doldrums to write family and friends far away. Or, send your yearly newsletter to them on another occasion, like their birthday or anniversary.

9. With the money you save from cutting down excess spending, invest in something for Christ. Give to an organization that helps the hungry and homeless. Set up a family "missionary bulletin board" in a conspicuous place like the kitchen. Post pictures of missionaries you support. If you don't yet help a specific missionary, make this the Christmas you start.

Traditions WITH A TWIST

When I discovered my oldest son's first-grade class had spent an entire week learning about Hanukkah, I went to the teacher and asked kindly if I could have time to tell her students the story of Christmas. I brought the Nativity set my mother-in-law had made for our family and allowed the children to handle it and ask questions.

Since that time, I've asked each of my children's teachers if I could come in and tell the Christmas story. Many people pray for me before, during, and after the date of my talks.

Last December I was allowed into five public-school classrooms to tell the Christmas story. Since my children are still young, I hope to be at the public school for many years to come, telling the wonderful and joyous story of our Savior's birth.

NANCY WHISMAN

"Aah . . . Don't you love these cozy winter nights—kids are asleep, hot chocolate, and a roaring fire on the VCR?"

Slow Down and Enjoy Yourself

SARA DUBOSE and DENISE TURNER

Holiday stresses got you down? The following five tips will help make your holidays less stressful.

1. Pick a date to complete your Christmas shopping and gift wrapping. Stick to it. When shopping is done, you will have time to volunteer with church projects, help the elderly plan and purchase gifts, visit the nursing home, or serve in other ways.

2. Examine your family traditions and expectations. Is it realistic to believe you can whip up gourmet delights for everyone on your gift list? Probably not. Substitute a quick, easy recipe and send it to a smaller number of friends.

Write down your special menus and purchase items early. If you have that extra dozen eggs or pound of flour on hand, you won't have to rush back to the grocery store. If you entertain, consider combining your party with a friend's party. It's half the work but all the fun.

3. Never forget that relationships are more important than mincemeat pie and twinkling lights. Set aside five or ten minutes a day to call somone who may be lonely, sick, forgotten, or worried. Your attention and concern may be his or her best Christmas present.

4. Say yes to rest and no to stress. You know your schedule and obligations better than anyone. Don't allow yourself to feel guilty when you have to say no to one more assignment.

Also, be sure to stick to your exercise routine and maintain good nutrition habits during the holiday. You'll have more energy.

5. Keep your quiet time. Nothing slows things down more than spending time with the Author of Peace. As you study and pray, ask God to teach you from his Word and help you share your faith during Christmas.

Christmas is so special to me because it's a time when everybody—whether they acknowledge it or not—celebrates the birth of Christ. The reason many are drawn to Christmas is because there's a deeper spiritual meaning to it. It's a time of hope and joy.

AMY GRANT

Legacy of Love

JANE LANDIN RAMIREZ

It was an early October morning—and as usual, I rushed about to get our second grader, Kevin, and fifth grader, Joe, ready for school and myself ready for work. Since my husband, Sandy, had the morning off, he was busy making breakfast for everyone.

"Daddy, can you take us to school today?" asked Kevin.

"'Fraid not, Bunbun. Your daddy's gonna work off some pounds today on his bike." He turned to me and winked. "I want that new suit your mom bought me to fit just right."

Sandy had just been promoted to assistant manager at work, and we were all proud of him. "Don't forget, I'm taking my special girl out tonight for a celebration dinner," he added.

Sandy had always been a romantic. He had won my heart our freshman year in high school with his homemade valentine, and twenty years later, he could still make me blush.

"'Bye, Dad. Be careful on your bike," said Joe, as we walked out to the car.

"See you soon! I love you," Sandy said, waving to us from the front door.

I dropped the boys off at school and hurried to the office. My morning was so busy, I decided to work through lunch. *Nothing's going to keep me from leaving on time today!* I thought.

But shortly before three o'clock, a coworker and close friend, Rose, entered my office. "Jane, there's been an accident," she said, ashen faced. "Sandy's at the hospital."

"How bad is it? Why didn't someone call me? What hospital is he at? Who called you?" I asked, panic-stricken.

"Calm down, Jane. I don't know how badly he's hurt. His boss called me. Someone from the hospital called him. I'll drive you there," she said.

My heart pounded as I went up to the front desk of the emergency room and asked to see my husband.

The attendant telephoned someone. "His wife is here," he said quietly, then turned to me. "Someone is coming to talk to you. Please wait here."

"Is he all right? Where is he? Can I see him?"

"Please wait here, ma'am. Someone will be here soon," he pleaded.

The hospital chaplain arrived and quietly ushered me into a private waiting room. "Your husband's been with us since nine-thirty this morning. We were told by the ambulance attendants he was hit by a car while riding a bicycle. The doctor will be here soon to talk to you. Is there someone I could call for you?"

This is a bad dream—I'll wake up from it soon, I thought, dazed and speechless. Just then, Rose entered the room. Her worried face triggered the tears I was fighting back. She sat me down and took over calling my family and our pastor. "Your sister is bringing the boys," she said.

I jumped to my feet when the doctor entered the room. "I'm Dr. Gray. Your husband is in ICU. I'm afraid the news isn't good. He suffered severe trauma to the head and spine. We had to amputate his left leg to control the bleeding. He's not breathing on his own, and the blood supply to his brain is about 2 percent of the normal level. His injuries were so severe, it's a miracle he's hung on as long as he has. I'm sorry—there's nothing more we can do."

My legs collapsed. I had to be helped to a chair. Anger and guilt consumed me, and I lashed out, "He's been alone all this time! Why did you wait so long to call me?"

The chaplain responded, "Your husband wasn't carrying any ID, so the police had only the initials from his high school ring to go on. One of our nurses identified him from the yearbook and remembered where he worked. His boss told us he would try to locate you. I'm sorry it took us so long to contact you."

"Please take me to him," I said, forcing down the lump in my throat.

"He never regained consciousness. His injuries have distorted his features, and all the tubing going through his body may be shocking," explained Dr. Gray.

"I need to see him right now," I insisted. I followed Dr. Gray. Tears welled in my eyes as I approached Sandy. I caressed his cold hands and gently kissed his forehead. "I'm here, my love. I'm so sorry that I didn't get here sooner," I said softly. Thoughts raced through my mind: *I'm so afraid—I don't know if I can go on without Sandy. I feel so alone. Please help me, Lord. Why did this have to happen? I feel so helpless. Dear God, please spare him any further suffering. Lord, help me to be strong for the boys.*

"I love you," I whispered. "You're in God's hands now." I so wanted Sandy to open his eyes and tell me everything would be all right.

Our silence was broken by a tap on my shoulder. Dr. Gray asked me to follow him. Outside the room were two other people.

"Mrs. Martinez, I know this is an extremely difficult time for you," said Dr. Gray. "I wish there were an easier way to do this, but there's very little time. Your husband's heart and other vital organs weren't injured by the accident, and there are two people here from an organ bank. They'd like a few minutes with you."

"Please, Dr. Gray, are you sure there's no hope?"

He replied sympathetically, "I wish I could tell you what you want to hear. Please listen to what these people have to say."

I'd never given organ donation any serious thought. Sandy and I'd never discussed it, and the idea was a bit frightening. But I listened as they gently asked me if we'd consider the possibility of donating Sandy's organs. Everything was happening so fast, I was relieved to see our pastor arrive.

Reverend O'Connor followed me into Sandy's room. "Sandy isn't going to make it, and those people were talking to me about donating his organs. I don't know what to do," I said.

"Jane, Sandy's work in the church exemplified his caring, giving nature. Remembering that may help you decide what to do. It's a decision, however, you shouldn't make alone. Do the boys know what's happening?" he added.

"No, they're on their way. I don't know how I'm going to explain all of this to them," I said as we both returned to the waiting room.

The crowded waiting room became a silent blur of faces when I entered. Two frightened little boys raced to me.

"Where's Daddy, Mommy? Why can't we see him?" they both asked.

I led them by the hand to Sandy's room. They stared at the figure on the bed as if he were a stranger. "Daddy is very hurt. He was struck by a car and thrown from his bike. He hit his head very hard. Don't be afraid."

We all huddled in a tight embrace, and I began, "Boys, the doctors have done everything to try to help him. We all love him very much, and I know you both want him to get better."

"Yes, Mommy, but how can we help him?" asked Kevin.

"The doctors can't help him, and we can't help him, but there is someone who can help him," I said.

"You mean God, don't you, Mommy?" asked Joe.

"Yes, God can help him, but to do that, he needs to take Daddy to heaven to live with him," I answered.

"But then we won't see him anymore, like Grandpa," sobbed Kevin.

"Daddy will always be with us, Kevin. He's in our hearts, and because we love him so much, we need to let him go to heaven where he won't hurt anymore. Grandpa's already in heaven, so Daddy won't be alone. Someday, when we go to heaven, we'll see both of them again," I explained.

"Do you remember how Daddy was always helping other people?" I added.

"Yes, Daddy liked helping people, even people he didn't know," added Kevin.

"Do you think Daddy would want to continue helping people if he could?" I asked.

"I guess so, but how, Mommy?" asked Joe.

"In heaven, God will give Daddy a new body that doesn't hurt, so he won't need his old body anymore. There are people we could help feel better if we gave them Daddy's beautiful green eyes or his great big heart," I explained.

"Will Daddy still love us even if he doesn't have his old heart? Will he still remember us?" questioned Kevin.

"Of course he will. Daddy will always love us no matter what happens," I answered.

After a brief silence, Kevin spoke. "Let's help those people, Mommy. Daddy would want us to."

Joe remained silent a few minutes longer. Cuddling his father's hand between his two small hands, he kissed it and whispered, "I love you, Daddy. Tell Grandpa I love him, too." Then he quietly slipped out of the room.

The rest of the family supported our decision without hesitation. My hands trembled as I signed the consent papers. After giving all the family some quick time alone with Sandy, the surgeons went to work to save all the organs possible.

As my sister drove me home, I thought of the celebration dinner that would never be and the new suit that would now be worn for the first and last time.

The healing process that followed was made easier with each letter we received from an organ bank. Although the identities of the recipients were concealed, we read about the high school principal who was within hours of dying until he received Sandy's heart. We heard from the kidney foundation about the two people who were now free from their dialysis machines. Two elderly persons received the gift of sight through cornea transplants. Sharing the letters with Kevin and Joe made it easier to talk about our loss.

Two months after the accident, we faced our first Christmas without Sandy. "Mommy, who's gonna put our Christmas lights up this year?" Kevin repeatedly asked.

I knew I couldn't disappoint the boys and break a family tradition of decorating our home with Christmas lights, but I just couldn't get into the Christmas spirit. Then it came—a letter from the organ tissue bank. As I read it aloud, the boys listened intently: "Your generous gift of life has shed light on the lives of some one hundred burn patients and their families, some with very severe skin burns."

"Mom, Daddy's been gone a long time, and he's still helping people," Joe said proudly.

"Mommy, I don't think that letter is right. Daddy was a very big man. I can't believe he only helped one hundred people. He probably helped at least a million!" Kevin added.

Memories of past Christmases flashed through my mind. Sandy always played Santa at our family gatherings. The old Santa suit didn't need much padding, and his naturally jolly cheeks and *ho ho ho*'s brought laughter to all. He would be missed deeply—particularly this first Christmas—and not only by his family. There'd be one less volunteer this year to deliver food and gifts to the needy or serve guests hot meals at the Ronald McDonald House. A beautiful sympathy card made and signed by the students from his Sunday school class reflected the love they had for their teacher. One child had written, "I am not going to be sad, because Mr. Martinez always made me laugh."

Christmas is a joyous season, I reflected. Like the child from his class, I, too, would refuse to be sad. Sandy had touched the lives of many—and even now his legacy of helping others was very much alive. I could not—and would not—let him down.

With renewed vigor, I exclaimed, "Boys, what do you say we get started on those lights and make Daddy proud of us, too!"

The cheerfulness and exuberant joy of Christmas paint the months of November and December with loud reds and fragrant greens. Yet in the midst of all this explosion of color, may our hearts turn toward the more "earthy" colors: God's birth among the straw and gentle animals and his continuing presence with us today.

RAMONA CRAMER TUCKER

Hassle-Free Shopping

KAREN HEFFNER

Do you feel overwhelmed by shopping? Then try these suggestions to make your next trip to the store or mall easier.

1. *Make a list early of those to whom you will give a gift.* Keep it in a place where you can easily jot down ideas. If you're assembling a gift—a basket with bath accessories, for instance—be sure to list each item you will need to purchase.

2. *Don't let the joy of gift giving be dampened months later because you're still paying off bills.* Set your gift budget in advance, and stick to it. Make sure the whole family follows the same policy.

3. *Wear comfortable clothes on your shopping trips.* Low-heeled shoes are a must! Arrive at the shopping center or mall shortly after it opens. You'll find ample parking, less frazzled clerks, and better merchandise displays. You'll have more energy, too. If you cannot shop during the day, plan to finish your shopping as early as possible in the season. Avoid shopping on weekends.

4. *Cut shopping expeditions into manageable blocks.* Plan your route (incorporating everyday shopping chores, if possible) and don't overdo. Stop for lunch or coffee, and go home *before* you're completely worn out.

5. *Be sure you understand the return policy wherever you shop.* If you're buying for faraway family or friends, consider shopping at a national chain to facilitate possible exchanges.

6. *Be alert to the hazards of shopping in crowds.* Lock parcels in the trunk, hang onto your purse, and ask for the carbons from your credit-card receipts.

7. *Use the Yellow Pages instead of running all over town looking for an item.* You can check prices and the availability of the item all at once.

8. *If you're looking for a specialty item or find it difficult to get out of the house, shop by mail.* Read descriptions carefully, and use a ruler, if necessary, to visualize sizes. Make sure you understand the refund/return policy, delivery time, and shipping costs.

9. *Some tips for next year: Pick up gifts during the year (especially on sale), but don't forget you have them!* Ask for gift boxes wherever they're offered. You won't have to stand in *that* line next year!

Christmas under Construction

KAREN BURTON MAINS, as told to Holly G. Miller

"Lord, if we are going to celebrate Christmas this year, many major miracles must occur!"

On Saturday morning, December 23, 1989, I was a woman who knew desperate straits when she saw them. Not a stick of furniture was in my dining or living rooms. Black plastic sheets hung over the entrances to the hallway and kitchen. Drywall lay in chunks on the floors, and a thick layer of white dust had settled on every household surface. Upstairs, bathroom floors had been ripped out, two toilets removed, and only one replaced.

This disruption was caused by the benevolence of a young pastor who had offered his help in fixing our various neglected household disasters.

Although things were a mess, I was *not* going to be daunted in my Christmas plans by a house in upheaval. I shopped for gifts, hosted a church youth Christmas party in the basement, and made frequent dashes to the hardware store for plumbing and building supplies.

By Saturday morning—the day before Christmas Eve—I surveyed the situation and began praying for a miracle. We had clearly gotten involved in too many projects. If Christmas that year had been up to me, our clan would have celebrated in some halfway fashion.

But what happened was like a miracle—everyone pitched in. All the family members at home dusted, scrubbed, vacuumed, hefted heavy furniture, toted lamps and pictures and knickknacks. One bathroom floor was finished upstairs, another toilet reinstalled. Errands were run, food was prepared, boxes were hauled from the attic, decorations were arranged throughout the house, and debris was whisked out of sight.

By the time our married children arrived home late Christmas Eve, our home shimmered with Christmas. The lanterns were aglow in the snow on the outside walk. The tree sparkled with its myriad of tiny lights. Wreaths had been hung on the stairways, while pink and cream-colored poinsettias peeked here and there from brass planters. Even the collection of Christmas books were in their baskets on the coffee table.

The miracle I experienced that Christmas of 1989 was one that always occurs when many hands, willing spirits, and eager workers labor together for a common goal. And in truth, this is what is always needed when we celebrate together the coming of Christ.

Having fun together during the holidays doesn't have to be work—
or take a lot of planning. Some of our most meaningful times occur during
the daily routines of life. We chase each other through the house with the dog;
we have tickle wars. We have family cleanup times, but we do it in
a fun way. I put on loud music and say, "OK, I don't like to do chores,
you don't like to do chores, but they've got to be done. So let's try to enjoy it."

KATHY PEEL

What's the Big Deal about Being a Christian?

MARIAN V. LIAUTAUD

Not long ago, my sister, Carole, called me long-distance to catch up. We talked about marriage, work, kids. But then, serendipitously, our conversation shifted to the topic of faith. "What's the big deal about being a Christian, anyway?" Carole asked me.

Her directness caught me off guard. I tried to share the reasons why it's important to make a decision for Christ, but I'm afraid my answer to life's most important question left her more befuddled than before she called.

Since our conversation, I've pondered Carole's question: What *is* the big deal about being a Christian? What difference has knowing the Lord made in my life? Although I always believed in God, it wasn't until I was twenty-three that I began asking questions like those my sister Carole is now asking. I kept meeting people who had devoted their lives to serving the Lord, and their relationship with Jesus gave them a peace and power I found irresistible.

Seven years ago, I finally accepted Jesus as my Savior. As I looked back on my excursion from nominal believer to committed Christian—and the ways my life has changed—it didn't take me long to come up with a list of reasons why I'm glad I'm a Christian.

No Sting in Death

When I was a sophomore in college, my father died. He had suffered the debilitating effects of lifelong diabetes, and for three years preceding his death, we watched his body deteriorate. Bit by bit, the man who had made a living as an artist lost the use of his hands, then his legs.

Once, about five years after my father died, I visited my mom at the house where I grew up. When I took my then two-year-old son, Danny, down into the basement where my dad had spent hours tinkering on model trains, I was suddenly struck with nostalgia. A memory of my dad hunched over his worktable—applying minidecals onto small-scale boxcars and erecting little villages with ant-sized people—flooded over me. The image was so real, I felt as if Dad were right there with us. Then I realized: He *is* still alive. John 11:25-26 says, "I am the resurrection and the life. He who believes in me will live, even though he dies; and whoever lives and believes in me will never die." My dad loved the Lord—and because he believed in Jesus, his spirit lives on forever.

Recently Danny, who is now eight, was asking me details about my dad's death. Though it makes me sad to think Danny and our two older sons will never know my dad in this world, I'm confident they will meet him in heaven someday. I'm glad I can temper the harshness of death for my sons with the reality of eternal life for those who believe in Christ.

The Gift of Peace

While the promise of eternal life is central to our faith, knowing Jesus isn't something we experience only in the future. He's present in our lives now, enabling us to live according to his will.

My husband, Dan, and I have been married just short of one decade. Between the two of us, we've held several jobs, most of them entrepreneurial-type self-employment. Never have we enjoyed financial stability, and there have been times when the pressure to meet our financial obligations was so intense Dan and I both felt as if we would crack. On top of frequent money problems, we have three active, growing boys and—up until this year—an old house in need of constant repair. The only way we've been able to maintain any semblance of serenity during these tumultuous times is

because we know the Lord and have seen his hand at work in our lives.

One of the most touching gestures of God's grace came a few years ago through my oldest sister, Laura. She knew the strain we were under financially. One day we were visiting at my mom's house, and as we were getting ready to say good-bye, she slipped me a few dollars to pick up milk and gas for the ride home. What might have seemed to her a simple act of kindness was a direct answer to my prayer that God would help meet our needs for the basic necessities.

Recognizing God's provision for both physical and emotional needs reassures me of his presence and gives me a peace only he offers. I'm glad I can claim the peace that surpasses all understanding, despite the circumstances I experience in the world.

Nearly eight years ago, a couple I know lost their son to suicide. Not surprisingly, this experience devastated them emotionally and spiritually. Why would a good God allow their son to take his own life? For months they immersed themselves in information about suicide, looking for clues to help them make sense of this tragedy. They harbored guilt and anger at themselves for missing the signs that pointed to their son's despair. And they wrestled with God over why he didn't intervene and save their son.

Finally, after working through the emotional and spiritual turmoil their son's death created, this couple came away with one kernel of truth that has sustained them: God never promises a pain-free life, but he does promise to always stay by our side. Knowing God is present in every situation gave this couple strength to move forward with their lives. Now they're using their experience to minister to others who face the tragedy of suicide.

Because Jesus lived and died on earth, he knows our pain. He stands beside us and endures every hardship with us. Believing in the Lord gives us an assurance of eternal life, but it also offers us the resources we need to make it through this world.

A Clean Slate

I grew up in the Catholic Church, and fourth grade marked the year of my first confession. After receiving intensive instruction, the day came when I waited in line to tell my sins to the priest. I had trouble understanding why I needed to confess my sins so often when I was ten years old, but now, at thirty-two, I realize how important it is to regularly examine my conscience and repent.

As I look at myself, I'm constantly humbled by my sinfulness. I assumed that once I had a personal relationship with Christ, I wouldn't struggle with so many of the same old sins like gossiping, yelling at my family, and making cutting remarks to my husband. While God has given me the strength to overcome some struggles—like worrying to excess about my weight—I have to ask for forgiveness every day for other failures. Thankfully, God "does not treat us as our sins deserve or repay us according to our iniquities. . . . As far as the east is from the west, so far has he removed our transgressions from us" (Ps. 103:10, 12).

My friend, Mary Ellen, concurs with my experience. "Sometimes I'm amazed at my own depravity. Even as a longtime Christian, I'm stunned by the sins I still commit. But I know that even when I sin, God's always there to forgive me. I don't deserve to be loved, yet he still forgives me and loves me."

A Purpose for Living

When I was a young girl, I used to sit on the curb at the end of our driveway and watch ants laboring to transport food from the street to their hill. It was there I first pondered the meaning of life. Even as a child, I sensed an underlying spiritual reality at work: Significance and purpose are possible only with

God. Without the Lord, people are no better off than those ants who work so hard only to die without reward for their efforts.

Though I've grown in my faith and have let go of faulty, childish perspectives, I've never changed my view on the fact that God creates each individual with a specific purpose for life. Margie, mother of five, shares this same sense of purpose as a Christian. "I don't have to spend my life wandering around, wondering who I am and what I'm here for," she says. "I have purpose because I know God has created me to do his work."

At this stage of Margie's life, serving God means devoting most of her time to raising her kids. For years I struggled with the issue of significance as a mother as I weaned myself from my full-time career. Finally I reached a point where I realized that if I shed all the roles I play, my ultimate job in this life is to reflect the living Christ within me.

Realizing this simple truth has given every job I do significance. Now, I spend the bulk of my working hours making sandwiches by my husband's side at our little sandwich shop. It's not the most glamorous work, but it earns us a living and gives us a chance to work with people who don't know the Lord.

Understanding God's will for us isn't always easy. But believing he is in charge and has a plan for us makes the journey worth traveling.

A Sense of Community

Last year, we moved to Minneapolis. For months I made few friends and wallowed in loneliness. Finally it occurred to me to pray to God to meet some Christian women. Within a few days I met Mary Ellen, then Esther, then Margie, all on the playground at my sons' preschool. None of them came right out and said, "Hi, I'm a Christian." But through casual conversation, we discovered we were believers, and that instant connection bonded us quickly.

When Mary Ellen and I talked over a cup of coffee for the first time, we revealed our struggles freely without fear of judgment. We know we share a God who forgives us. My budding friendship with Mary Ellen has made me thankful I can connect with another woman on a spiritual level and in the process be touched by the Spirit through her insight and caring.

For every Christian friend we make, we possess a new opportunity to know the Lord through that person's eyes. My friend Margie says, "Believing in Christ gives me a sense of belonging. I belong to the family of God to have fellowship with the Father." When you're friends with other believers, you're striving for the same goal: to know the Lord better and to uphold each other in the quest to imitate Christ's love.

Absolutes in an "Anything Goes" World

When you watch too much evening news, it's easy to start wringing your hands over the state of our nation. Like most Americans, I'm continually discouraged by our apparent lack of morals and values.

In the small sandwich shop my husband and I opened recently, we work with mostly twenty-something men and women. To hear them talk, you get a picture of a generation largely devoid of absolutes. As one of our employees says about his peers, "We have no boundaries. Everything is 'normal' and acceptable, so no one holds us accountable for wrong behavior."

Hearing this employee's assessment of many who live in the nineties makes me glad I have the Bible to direct me. God's Word truly is "a lamp to my feet and a light for my path" (Ps. 119:105). Through Scripture, God sets the standard by which we are to live. He spells out right from wrong, and I'm constantly accountable to him for my actions. If ever there was a "how

to" book on life, the Bible is it. I'm glad God took the time to publish it.

Hope in the Midst of Sadness

The first Christmas after my dad died was the loneliest season of my life. While everyone around me was making merry, I felt weighed down with sadness. One Sunday during Advent, as I sat in church alone, mulling over the meaning of Christmas in the light of my sorrow, it hit me: Christmas is about *hope.* The carved image of Jesus in the manger is a reminder that God loves us so much, he used extreme measures to gain fellowship with us. The Christ child is our ultimate hope for knowing God now—and forever.

That Christmas, though marked by deep grief, was one of the most meaningful ones I've ever celebrated. For the first time I realized how glad I was to be a Christian. I don't have to relegate the season's meaning to December 25. As a believer, I can enjoy Christmas every day. Through the infant Jesus, I'm reminded of the hope for salvation and eternal life his presence in the world offered then and today.

Christ is God's ultimate gift to us. I think I'll call my sister, Carole, and share it with her.

Traditions WITH A TWIST

Every Christmas morning, before we open our gifts, our family reads the story of Jesus' birth from the book of Luke (2:1-20). To keep the story lively, we switch Scripture versions each year. The "newest" family member has the honor of reading the story. Sometimes that means it's read by a child; other times by a visitor. One year, an exchange student from Germany was living with us. She read the story first in German, then translated it into English from her German Bible. Hearing the age-old story in different ways helps us focus our holiday on what Christmas is really about—Christ's birth and the joy and hope that it brings to humankind.

TRICIA ALBERT

Taking the Long View

RAMONA CRAMER TUCKER

As I think back over my favorite Christmases, several scenes come to mind:

- Arriving home from my first lonely semester of college to the aroma of ginger cookies baking and the warmth of my parents' hugs.
- The clicking of cameras as my roommates and I celebrated Christmas around our tiny tree, for what we thought would be our last time together. One of us had been diagnosed with lymphoma and wasn't expected to live (but, by God's grace, twelve years later she's doing well).
- The Christmas two friends joyfully burst in at midnight to announce their engagement.
- The year I couldn't go home to my family because I'd had my wisdom teeth pulled. That Christmas morning a friend sacrificed the remainder of his family celebration to drive to my apartment and feed me Jell-O and chicken soup. In the process, he began to fall in love with me . . . and he's now been my husband for ten years!

Frankly, I didn't think any Christmases could top those in lasting memories. But this last difficult Christmas has made a deep impression on me that won't be easily forgotten.

As an on-the-go person, I've always found it difficult to just sit and enjoy God's presence. It's far easier—and more fun—for me to continually *do* things for him: bake cookies to encourage a coworker who's down, scrub a friend's floor when she comes home from the hospital with a new baby, grocery shop for an elderly neighbor. Although it's good and right to do things for others, reaching out in friendship in the name of Christ, at times I go into "overdrive mode," getting myself into so many activities that I wear myself out.

This last Christmas, my overbusy lifestyle caught up with me. I came down with pneumonia and spent six weeks in bed, unable to do anything celebratory to make the holidays special. All my best-laid plans, my to-do lists, my great-gift ideas came to an abrupt halt. For the first few weeks I was too sick to care. But as I began to recover, so did my "do something" spirit. Yet in my physical weakness, I discovered I couldn't do anything—I could barely get out of bed without help. I'd worn myself so ragged that my body had finally revolted and said "Enough is enough!"

After that bout with illness, I realized I needed to make some changes in my lifestyle to keep me healthy both physically and spiritually . . . and I have (although my "do everything" personality still takes over at times!).

As you head into your Christmas holidays, how's your pace? Do you, like me, tend to run from activity to activity, trying to be all things to all people? If so, you may be on your way to "Holiday Burnout." As I lay quietly in bed, I had plenty of time to brainstorm how *not* to do the holidays the same way again. Maybe the tips I discovered will help you avoid holiday burnout, too:

- Focus on people, not things. Give others the gift of your *presence*, not your presents.
- Be realistic about what you can and can't do with the time and energy you have.
- Remember that a plate of homemade goodies (low-fat for those watching calories and cholesterol) can say "I care" as much as an expensive gift.
- Share with others what Christmas is all about—the great gift of God's love.
- And, most important, give your Creator the time and attention he deserves.

While sick in bed, I was quiet long enough to discover that prayer is not only talking, but *listening*. God wants a *relationship* with us. How true the lines of Christina Rossetti's poem are:

> *What can I give Him*
> *Poor as I am;*
> *If I were a shepherd,*
> *I would bring a lamb;*
> *If I were a wise man,*
> *I would do my part.*
> *But what can I give Him?*
> *I will give my heart.*

Simply put, that's what God asks for: our heart. In the busyness of the holidays, God wants to give you the awesome and comforting gift of his presence. Will you accept it, in the midst of this season of hurry and color and celebration?

Remember that the promises of eternity began with Christ's birth to two common-place people in a simple stable with an animal's feeding trough as a bed and star-struck shepherds as visitors. The creator of the universe became human for us so that we might experience a relationship and everlasting life with him. Now *that's* the true meaning of Christmas—a Christmas we can celebrate year round.

Special Ways to Focus on Christ's Birth

Personal Goals for the Coming Year

Acknowledgments

Today's Christian Woman magazine and Tyndale House Publishers would like to thank the following people, who graciously gave their permission to use the following material from *Today's Christian Woman* in this book.

Arias, Pamela. "Spiritual Gifts" (November/December 1995).

Barker, Debbie L. "Hope for the Holiday Weary" (November/December 1991).

Beaderstadt, Barbara. "Home Cooking" (November/December 1994).

Belsaas, Marsha. "Norwegian Noel" (November/December 1995).

Bence, F. Evelyn. "Center Christmas on Christ" (November/December 1986).

Bence, Kathy. "What about Hanukkah?" and "Celebrate Advent at Home" (November/December 1986); "Making Guests Feel at Ease" and "Mother's Little Helpers" (November/December 1987).

Burleson, Marion. "Hugs Given Here" from "How I Share My Faith on the Job" (September/October 1994).

Clark, Marilyn. "Jam Session" (November/December 1994).

Collier, Diana. "Letter Legacy" (November/December 1994).

Crockett, Marsha. "Quick & Easy Holiday Favorites" and "Gifts of the Spirit" (November/December 1989).

Denight, Alison. "Holiday Hand-Me-Downs" (November/December 1991).

Erwin, Kathie. "Moo Testament" (November/December 1993).

Ewart, Paula R. "Camp Christmas" (November/December 1995).

Hallgren, Judy D. "Renewed Vows" (November/December 1994).

Hardie, Michele. "All Is Calm" (November/December 1993).

Harmon, Debbie. "Getting Her Goat" (November/December 1994).

Heffner, Karen. "Alone for the Holidays" and "Hassle-Free Shopping"

(November/December 1986); "Happy Get-Togethers" (November/December 1989); "A Date with My Calendar" (November/December 1990).

Higgs, Liz Curtis. "The Ever-Ready Christmas Tree" (November/December 1994).

Huseman, Roxanne. "Life-Sized Love" (November/December 1994).

Jackson, Kathy. "Band of Gold" (November/December 1994).

Kindig, Eileen Silva. "Family Stories" (November/December 1992).

Langberg, Dr. Diane Mandt. "We Have Different Views of the Holidays" from "My Husband Hates the Holidays" (November/December 1991); "Whose Home for the Holidays?" (November/December 1995).

Liautaud, Marian V. "What's the Big Deal about Being a Christian?" (November/December 1995).

Mains, Karen Burton, as told to Holly G. Miller. "Christmas under Construction" (November/December 1992).

Marret, Bonnie C. Contributed "Elves Sightings" (November/December 1995).

Marusich, Kristen. "Grandma's Bequest" (November/December 1994).

Mason, Babbie, as told to Holly G. Miller. "The Last Christmas" (November/December 1992).

Mathers, Mayo. "A Gift Worth Repeating" (November/December 1995); "I Didn't Want to Share My Mom" (November/December 1995).

Meece, Debbie, as told to Holly G. Miller. "Gift Horse" (November/December 1992).

Miller, Holly G. "25 Gifts You'll Love to Give . . . and They'll Love to Get" (November/December 1995).

Miller, Judy. "Handmade Treasures" (November/December 1994).

Mittelstaedt, Elizabeth. "The Wish List" (November/December 1994).

Montoya, Cindy. "Pajama Party" (November/December 1995).

Nelson, Denise. "Beast Feast" (November/December 1995).

Newenhuyse, Elizabeth Cody. "Calories Don't Count When . . ." (November/December 1994).

Patterson, Lauretta. "No Time to Entertain" (January/February 1991).

Ramirez, Jane Landin. "Legacy of Love" (November/December 1995).

Reisser, Dr. Paul. "Christmas Cautions" from "Healthy Holidays to You" (November/ December 1993).

Rollins, Catherine E. "10 Things You Can Say to Make Someone's Day" (May/June 1992).

Saxman, Marcene Y. "Surprise Santa" (November/December 1994).

Silvious, Jan. "'Tis the Season of Sibling Stress," taken from "Your Siblings, Yourself" (November/December 1990).

Sneed, Drs. Sharon and David. "Lighten Up! . . . the Holiday Weight-Gain Roller Coaster" (November/December 1992).

Standard, Bonnie. "The Gift of Life" (November/December 1994).

Struck, Jane Johnson. "Rachael Crabb: Hospitality on the Run" (January/February 1992); "Entertaining with Style" (November/December 1987); "Getting Your Husband to Help" (November/December 1987); "Win the Prize for 'Best Guest'" (November/December 1987).

Thomas, Terri L. "Decades of Friendship" (November/December 1994).

Tucker, Phyllis. "Back to the Bible" (November/December 1994).

Tucker, Ramona Cramer. "The Christmas I Spent with Strangers" from "Between Friends" (November/December 1995).

Turner, Denise. "Slow Down and Enjoy Yourself" with Sara DuBose (November/ December 1986); "Old-Fashioned Advice for Today" (November/December 1987); "When You Can't Go Home" (November/December 1989).

Ward, Sherri. "Belated Barbie" (November/December 1994).

Weaver, Ginger. "Advent of Friendship" (November/December 1995).

Whisman, Nancy. "I Love to Tell the Story" (November/December 1995).

Wilcox, Barbara. "Door to Door" (November/December 1994).

Zornes, Jeanne. "Did $omebody $ay Chri$tma$?" (November/December 1986).

Cartoon Illustrations:

The cartoons on pages 25, 34, 47 used by permission of Martha F. Campbell.

The cartoons on pages 29, 94, 104 used by permission of David W. Harbaugh.

The cartoon on page 33 used by permission of Patrick Hardin.

The cartoons on pages 9, 65, 131 used by permission of John McPherson.

The cartoons on pages 15, 70, 78, 105, 120, 127 used by permission of Rick Stromoski.

The cartoon on page 48 used by permission of Fred H. Thomas.